MW00629165

PRAISE FOR

DIVERGE

"*Diverge* is a great exploration of a new angle to accelerate the next level of performance of your business and leadership…a must-read for every leadership team."

– **DOM CECERE,** C-Suite | Executive Positions, KB Home, Owens Corning, Honeywell International Inc.

"A powerful reminder and actionable playbook for rising from the sea of sameness…to propel your company toward its greatest potential."

– **HAMID GHANADAN,** Founder of Linus, Author of *Persuading Scientists*

"A strong reminder of how driving different thinking through an organization can provide a fresh perspective and drive stronger results."

– **DICK LANTZ,** Executive Vice President | General Manager, Roofing & Insulation Supply

"Bill presents a novel approach to conducting business and makes 'thinking out of the box' a useful reality. The book will remain on my shelf as an annual 'must-read'."

– **BOB FRANCO,** CEO | Principal, Invictus Consulting LLC

"*Diverge* focuses on creating a 'unique and different' value proposition to transform a business, rather than simply managing what already exists for a more prosperous future."

– **CHUCK JERASA,** Group President, Gibraltar Building Products

1

"Bill continually provides insights that challenge the status quo and create true differentiation for clients. Use these insights to challenge your current SOPs and find your .1% solution."

– **STEVE LYNCH,** President, Clopay Building Products

"Bill demonstrates how good companies can become great companies by expanding their value proposition and leveraging new thinking throughout their organization."

– **DEE SLATTERY,** Senior Director of Global Brand Marketing, Ansell

"Bill creatively identifies how business leaders can implement these strategies and succeed. Helping you look at your company and business in a different way that will cause it to prosper."

– **LEON GAROUFALIS,** President | COO, Composites One

"Bill has an incredible ability to successfully mix logic with creativity to produce superior results. This book provides unique insights that can be applied to your environment."

– **FRED DANNHAUSER,** President, Quaker Manufacturing Corporation

"Full of insightful approaches that will help look at business at a different angle. The case studies and concepts provide strong takeaways to help drive enhanced business performance."

– **ERIC NILSSON,** Retired VP Corporate Marketing, CertainTeed Corporation

"*Diverge* shows how 'business as usual' can take over and handcuff a category and the companies serving it. I took away several valuable concepts that I plan to utilize."

– **STEVE STEPHENS,** Vice President, Four Seasons Remodeling

"Bill has always had a pioneering approach and I have witnessed the success of many of his unique insights and strategies. It's great to see them all come together in *Diverge.*"

– **MARK MONTGOMERY,** Vice President of Marketing, Ply Gem Windows

"A must-read if you're looking to add new blood and thinking to your company's strategy and staff. For companies looking to lead differently, *Diverge* gives you strong concepts to live by."

– **CARL LARSON,** Business Development Manager, Hillyard Inc.

"Bill is a true thought leader that has enabled him to deliver extraordinary business results in every role. *Diverge* is a great culmination of his insights and proven business approach."

– **JIM DENNY,** Vice President Sales, Huber Engineered Wood

"*Diverge* succinctly defines a plan on how to drive yourself and your team to optimize business performance. Read it, and push yourself and your team to someplace uncomfortable."

– **GLEN HIRSCHFELD,** President, Power Brushes Inc.

"A valuable business book for any size business or industry you play in. Bill provides great examples and immediately usable concepts that will help drive enhanced profitability."

– **JOHN BAILEY,** Director of Marketing and Sales, Environmental Stoneworks

"*Diverge* is a collection of Bill's unique approach. It's great to see how these all come together. If you want amazing results, have your team read it!"

– **JEFF HIRE,** President, Installed Building Products

"Rossiter reminds us that it's truly unique differentiators that take modern companies from good to great. His perspectives help business leaders find and leverage their unique value."

– **CHRISTIAN NOLTE,** Vice President of Marketing, Henry

"Rossiter explains simple yet distinct business approaches that force you to think, make decisions, lead, and take actions differently. A great read for leaders in any market!"

– **TODD H. HALL,** President, Concrete Cutting & Finishing Division, Blount International

"*Diverge* will give you and your team the perspective and the processes to positively impact your business results. A practical approach to turning the aspirations into actual core values."

– **ROBERT BROCKMAN,** Director of Marketing, Armstrong Floors

"A breath of fresh air for any business that is looking to shake itself out of the 'sea of sameness' and create a strategic position for itself in the marketplace."

– **DAN HENNE,** Director of Marketing, University of Michigan

"Simple, yet very profound. Bill defines how leaders can differentiate themselves and their businesses in a way that positively and exponentially adds value to our customers. Powerful."

– **DEREK PAULSEN,** Group Vice President, Gibraltar Industries, Inc.

"*Diverge* presents thought-provoking approaches to managing in today's rapidly changing environment. Read it and challenge yourself and then the thinking of everyone on your team."

– **CARL HEDLUND,** Retired CEO, Therma-Tru Doors / Operating Partner, Hudson Ferry Capital LLC

DIVERGE

STAND OUT IN A SEA OF SAMENESS

BILL ROSSITER

Hooley Publishing
Sylvania, OH

ISBN: 978-0-9993641-1-6

Illustrations by Phil Graves, cover design by Anita Holman, interior layout by JPL Design Solutions, 1st edition edited by Michael Dowling, 2nd edition edited by Ashley McMahon.

Printed and bound in the United States of America
Cataloging-in-Publication data is on file with The Library of Congress

Rossiter, Bill.
Diverge: Stand Out in a Sea of Sameness
– 2nd ed.

To my mother, Mary Jane, who was in hospice as I was finishing this book. I wrote the last few chapters while sitting by her side. She taught me the power of speech and words, and, most importantly, she taught me how to lead with care.

Two roads diverged in a wood, and I—
I took the one less traveled by,
And that has made all the difference.

Robert Frost
"The Road Not Taken"

TABLE OF CONTENTS

diverge (v) to separate from the usual route; to create a new path in a different direction

ACKNOWLEDGEMENTS

I am extremely grateful to the many people who have positively impacted my life, both professionally and personally, in ways that have helped to make this book a reality. First and foremost, I would like to thank all of the business mentors who have helped shape my thoughts and my approach to business and leadership throughout my career. Any success and breadth of opportunity I have enjoyed would not have been possible without their guidance and encouragement. Their mentorship and dedication to my success has fueled my ongoing commitment to mentor others in their pursuit of excellence.

I also wish to express my appreciation to my team at Interrupt. Several years ago, I left Corporate America with the vision of creating an exceptional organization with amazing people dedicated to the success of outstanding client partners. I consider myself extremely fortunate that this vision has become a reality. What a blessing it is today to lead such a dedicated, smart, and passionate team in the creation of an organizational culture that measures its success by the success of those it serves.

During the long hours of work and travel throughout the more than 30 years of my career, my family could not have supported me more patiently and lovingly. I am deeply indebted to them for bearing with me, especially over these past few months as I devoted additional time to writing this book.

Thank you very much, Michael Dowling, for doing such an outstanding job shepherding me through the creation of this book. You have made the writing process enjoyable and the final product professional.

Finally, I wish to acknowledge you, the reader. I commend you for your desire to increase your knowledge and your success. I have been blessed in my professional life with strong support systems and sound guidance. I hope you are enjoying the same in your career, and if not, I hope you will seek them. In the pages of this book, I have passed on to you some of the things I have learned over the years. My goal is to encourage you and give you additional perspectives, so you will be more successful than you previously thought possible.

PREFACE

If you change the way you look at things,
the things you look at change.
–Wayne Dyer

My goal in writing this book is to challenge you to break away from the traditional tried-and-true approaches you've been using to lead your business. I want to push you to diverge from the typical and reach for the exceptional. The concepts presented in these pages will enable you to view your business differently and lead it more powerfully. My conviction, based on years of management and consulting experience with all types of companies, is that

[
...thinking and leading from
a fresh and focused
perspective will enable
you to dramatically enhance
your business results.
]

thinking and leading from a fresh and focused perspective will enable you to dramatically enhance your business results.

As leaders, we tend to make business more complex than it needs to be. We busy ourselves with non-critical tasks, and we keep doing them year after year without stepping back to consider whether there's a different way that will deliver optimal and even incredible results. When you wipe away the truly unimportant items and dare to think and act differently, making money in business can be simple.

Typically, very little original thinking goes on in businesses and the industries they serve. There is a sea of sameness that permeates every industry. Competitors in the same industry sell basically the same types of products through the same types of channels to the same types of customers using the same types of approaches. Their teams sit around their respective conference tables month after month discussing the same types of issues and making the same types of decisions. Year after year, there's very little substantive change in their business or industry.

Does this sound familiar? More to the point, does this describe your company? My experiences with other businesses tell me that if you take a hard, honest look, you will have to admit that to a large extent it does.

But your company doesn't have to stay stuck in this "sea of sameness." You can break free of routinized thinking and begin to think and act differently. Companies that make the effort to intentionally diverge from the norm invariably come up with ideas and strategies that accelerate their growth and propel them ahead of their competitors. In this book, I will tell you how to capitalize on this profit-enhancing approach.

A Bit About My Background

Before you consider the ideas I present in this book, you deserve to know something about my background. It has been my good fortune to hold numerous positions that have contributed to my leadership and business acumen. Of utmost importance has been the support I have received from several mentors who have shaped my thinking and my approach to business.

For as long as I can remember, I have been passionate about and proficient at helping businesses become more profitable. A job with a remodeling contractor in the Philadelphia area during high school gave me my initial taste of business. While doing everything from marketing and selling to generating leads and swinging a hammer, I learned about all aspects of running a small business. Transitioning to college, I helped put myself through the University of Notre Dame by providing marketing and consulting services to all of the university's student-run stores and to small businesses in the Indiana area.

Upon graduation, I immediately joined Owens Corning, a highly respected Fortune 500 company in the building materials industry. During the next 21 years, I took on rapidly increasing management responsibilities in all areas of the corporation. When leadership noticed that I had exceptional skills for seeing things differently—and for making money (a great skill to have!)—they began sending me out to fix ailing divisions, start new business models, and open new channel approaches. From these opportunities, I learned a great deal about how to lead people, processes, and businesses. The most important thing I learned was how to approach things totally differently. How to break away from the norm. Through all of this, I became proficient at encouraging my teams to think and act differently.

My final and most rewarding assignment was as Director of Demand Creation. The goal of demand creation is to create larger demand for an entire category or industry. It's about making the entire pie bigger, rather than simply taking a bigger piece of the existing pie. To grow demand, you must think about your industry and the world differently. Companies that create new demand can reap huge rewards because they can usually capture a disproportionately large percentage of that newly created demand. In this book, you will learn how to profit from this dynamic growth concept.

A Different Kind of Ad Agency

To illustrate the power of thinking differently, I'll tell you a bit more of my personal story. In 2007, I left Owens Corning to purchase Interrupt, a successful marketing firm that was serving Fortune 1000 companies in the building materials industry. Prior to my investment, this marketing agency had functioned like most others. It specialized in producing promotional campaigns and other "pretty stuff" to help its clients sell more of their products.

People warned me against purchasing an agency, especially one that was so heavily concentrated in the construction industry. At this time, the new construction sector of the economy was just heading into a 75% downturn, and our firm's clients had cut way back on their marketing expenditures. The industry pie was getting smaller, so there were no longer enough marketing dollars to keep all of the existing agencies in business. The decline forced me to begin thinking differently about our business and how we might best serve our clients.

When I looked at the situation through fresh eyes, I realized that our prospective clients really needed increased profitability, not catchy marketing campaigns. They required strategic guidance about where to take their business and how to leverage their existing assets.

I couldn't satisfy that need by concentrating simply on the promotional aspects of marketing. So, after assessing our firm's particular core competencies, we transitioned from a typical marketing agency to a specialized strategic branding and marketing firm. We repositioned ourselves from being a mere "vendor" of marketing services, which simply helped our clients promote their products, to being a trusted business partner providing research, innovative insights, strategic marketing advice, channel strategies assistance, and branding services that enabled our clients to differentiate themselves and better position their company and products in the marketplace. Our goal was to help them spot promising gaps, seize new opportunities, outperform the market, and optimize their profitability by viewing their industry and their business differently.

In order to fulfill our newly defined mission, we had to deepen our knowledge of our clients' businesses. We learned which aspects of their operations contributed most to profits and why. We studied how their competitors went to market, what gaps in their industry were ripe to be filled, what trends were influencing their niche of the industry, and what results their board of directors and stockholders expected. To gain this knowledge, we had to become intimately familiar with the details of their operations, all the way down to understanding their profitability profile by SKU, geo zone, customer type, and channel. We had to clearly understand how our clients defined what success meant to them and their stakeholders.

Perfect Timing

The 75% slump in the new construction market meant that

three-quarters of our clients' resources were either underutilized or not utilized at all. Therefore, instead of trying to sell standard promotions and marketing services, as other agencies were doing, we helped our clients increase profits by offering them strategic advice about alternative channels for employing their underutilized assets. For example, we helped many clients evaluate new market opportunities, and we provided them with the new branding approaches and sales and marketing tools they needed to perform well with these different audiences and markets.

Ours was the perfect approach for this down market. People were looking for strategic solutions, and we became the expert strategic partners for their business. After they had benefited from our insights and strategic planning solutions, they came to us for branding and marketing services to execute these new strategies. Initially, our clients didn't spend much on marketing since the market was weak. But when the market began to rebound, and as our marketing initiatives demonstrated strong ROI in the marketplace, they began to invest more with us.

Our clients came to view us as a trusted business partner because we treated their business results as our own. We were the only marketing and branding firm in North America that talked with its clients about their capacity utilization and other business triggers. We would ask questions such as, "If we could help you increase your capacity utilization by 5%, how much would that boost your bottom line?"

Even a small percentage increase in utilization can dramatically increase profits and profit margins by spreading fixed costs. For example, when we worked with a client to pinpoint how a 2% increase in utilization in their Midwest plant could push $2.5 million additional to their bottom line, that client was easily able to justify an expenditure of $250,000 for our business guidance and the resulting marketing services to help them realize a sustainable 2% utilization gain. Other firms that were merely selling $250,000 in advertising programs had a much harder time because they didn't understand their clients' triggers to profitability, and therefore they didn't know how their clients should invest money in marketing to make more money. Since our competitors didn't address their prospects' triggers to profitability, they couldn't sell their services based on ROI. In contrast, we always talked about and demonstrated marketing dollars as "investments" rather than as costs or expenditures.

Although the marketing and branding campaigns we created for our clients won numerous awards, we gauged our success solely by how much we helped our clients differentiate their brand in a cluttered industry. Our ultimate goal was to help our clients outperform industry benchmarks. As they prospered, we prospered. While other agencies were stagnating or going out of business, our firm was achieving double-digit growth year after year. New clients and even private equity firms looking for strong industry knowledge and a business partnership approach to marketing and branding began seeking us out. I'm sharing this story not to toot our own horn, but to illustrate the power of living the principles that I will present in this book.

Profit Sharing

You will be most successful when you push yourself and your team to diverge from the typical and begin to think dramatically differently about your

> You will be most profitable when you align and define your success in terms of your customers' success.

business, your industry, and your possibilities. You will be most profitable when you align and define your success in terms of your customers' success.

In *Diverge,* I tell you how to craft, enroll, and execute within this win-win strategy. After you have read this book, I hope you will refer to it again and again. To enhance its value as a reference, we've included the Glossary section in the back.

If you're a leader who wants to improve your personal performance and the profitability of your company or department, you and your team will benefit from reading this book. I believe it will open your eyes to new and unrealized opportunities in your marketplace. My desire is that upon finishing it you will say, "This book has given me the guidance, inspiration, and motivation I need to find my uniqueness and change my perception of my business and my industry. It has challenged me to diverge from the ordinary and pursue the extraordinary."

1

DEFINING YOUR DIFFERENCE

Discovery consists of seeing what everybody has seen and
thinking what nobody has thought.

–Albert Szent-Gyorgi

People come in all shapes and sizes. Some are short, others are tall. Some are slim, others are heavy. Some have brown hair, others have black hair, blonde hair, red hair... or no hair! And if you could get to know all of these people, you would invariably find that they possess remarkably different personalities, temperaments, habits, values, opinions, and aspirations.

Yes, we humans are very different from one other. But actually, the similarities are far greater than the differences. For one thing, each of us—that includes every one of the over seven billion people on Earth—shares DNA that is 99.9% identical! This means that our individual differences are, to a significant degree, determined by only .1% of our DNA.

There's a lot we don't know about DNA, but we do know it's the sole communicator of genetic instructions determining how our body functions. It has considerable influence over our appearance, thoughts, actions, and worldview. It even plays a major role in shaping our ultimate life outcomes. The .1% of our DNA that creates our uniqueness is at the core of our personal identity.

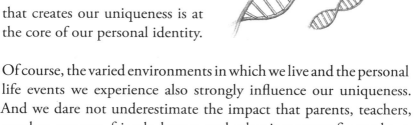

Of course, the varied environments in which we live and the personal life events we experience also strongly influence our uniqueness. And we dare not underestimate the impact that parents, teachers, coaches, spouses, friends, bosses, and other important figures have on our life. But these experiences and influences must all run through the filter of our DNA.

From the Body to the Board Room

In some ways, companies are like humans. You might say that each organization has its own DNA, composed of its mission, values, experiences, policies, procedures, customs, priorities, and other key attributes. This business DNA plays a major role in determining the organization's path and culture. It also dramatically impacts the value the company delivers to its employees and customers, which to a large degree, determines the business's ultimate success.

Going one step further with our analogy, the differences between companies, like the differences between humans, appear on the surface to be substantial. And as business leaders, isn't this what we want to believe? We take pride in thinking that our own company is rather exceptional. This view gives us hope (usually false hope) that we can easily deliver the results we boldly project in our strategic plans.

But my experience with hundreds of businesses in scores of industries has convinced me that actually the differences between companies are minimal. In fact, I would argue that the organizational DNA of companies, like the DNA in humans, is 99.9% identical. Most organizations, especially those in the same industry, tend to allow themselves to be sucked in to the sea of sameness. They manufacture the same types of products, hire the same kinds of people, espouse the same kinds of values, develop the same types of goals and objectives, spend time on the same kinds of issues, make the same types of decisions, and ultimately make the same kinds of mistakes. If you were able to spend a day sitting in on management meetings and roaming the halls of several of your competitors, I believe you would be surprised at the similarity of the discussions, challenges, opportunities, decisions, and business results.

> If your company is going to escape from the false security of this "sea of sameness" and excel, it needs to be different—genuinely different—from the other companies in your industry.

If your company is going to escape from the false security of this "sea of sameness" and excel, it needs to be different—genuinely different—from the other companies in your industry. That's not to disparage the 99.9% of your DNA that is similar to other organizations. It provides a necessary platform for your operations. But to outperform your competitors and your industry as a whole, you need to harness the power of your organization's unique DNA.

Just as a .1% variance in human DNA can create remarkably different characteristics in people, a mere .1% variance in business DNA can dramatically differentiate your company. Successful companies fully embrace their .1% to guide their business. Your challenge is to identify the unique .1% that is relevant to the audiences you are attempting to engage, embed it into your organization's culture, develop your overall strategy to leverage it out to the market, and dynamically execute that strategy.

Your Reason to Exist

Earlier in my career, when I worked for Owens Corning, one of my general management responsibilities with the businesses I led was to develop the strategic plan for the coming one to three years. When I presented my plan to the CEO, Dave Brown, he would invariably ask me a simple but powerful question that forced me to strip the discussion down to the very core of my strategy. He would say, "What is your reason to exist?" By that he meant, "Are the new ideas you are proposing about products, markets, and marketing approaches really different and relevant, or are they just improvements on things that we or our competitors are already doing? What does your approach offer that the market really needs to be more successful? What does it provide that our customers can't live without?"

He didn't use the term "unique .1%," but that's essentially what he meant. He was telling us to stop thinking about how we could tweak our existing products and services and start thinking about innovative ideas. He was challenging us to develop innovative insights from market trends in our industry, the needs of our customers and their customers, the gaps in the overall marketplace, and the trends in industries that were more advanced than ours. The next part of our challenge was to envision new products, services, and market approaches aligned with these insights.

When I could persuade my CEO that my team's strategic plan would dramatically help our customers achieve greater success and that our proposed products and services had a truly unique reason to exist, it was relatively easy to secure the requested funding. We didn't need to spend hours producing 100 pretty, fact-filled PowerPoint slides to convince the board of directors. Just a dozen slides that told my reason to exist attached to a description of the opportunity were sufficient. As we will discuss in Chapter 4, PowerPoint slides have become a crutch for many managers throughout Corporate America. They actually hamper your ability to communicate your strategic path and the rationale behind it in a five-minute conversation, which should be your goal.

A product has a unique "reason to exist" when your customers truly need that product in order to be more successful. Developing the rationale for a "reason to exist" seems like a simple concept, but as a good friend once told me, "Simple ain't always easy!" To envision these new ideas and approaches, we had to spend more time thinking differently and developing original and unheard-of insights about our industry, our company, and our customers. As we'll discuss in Chapter 6, we had to move from focusing on the urgent items that usurped our time to focusing on the critical items that leveraged our uniqueness and delivered extraordinary business results.

Looking for Your Unique .1%

You might be wondering, how do I find my company's unique .1%? When we go in to consult with a client, we talk with the company's team members at different levels and in different functional areas to see what buried treasures we can uncover. In some cases, we'll find tremendous potential in a new technology that's lying dormant. We may discover unappreciated organizational expertise, a new product idea the company hasn't leveraged out to market, an existing process that hasn't been implemented, or a new marketing approach that hasn't been tried. Sometimes we find that the folks in R&D have proprietary expertise, processes, research findings, or product ideas that could deliver significant impact to customers and substantial profits to the company, but nobody in sales, marketing, or general management is even aware of them.

When company leaders open their eyes and start asking different questions, they are invariably amazed at the number of game-changing ideas that surface from under their noses. Many of these ideas might have lain around the company for years, but they have remained unnoticed because leaders have not asked questions from a different angle that would evoke different answers. Most of the time that's because leaders have not taken the time to pull back from the urgency of the day to see the industry and their organization from a fresh, nontraditional perspective. Leaders who need to be viewed as the smartest person in the room hamper the growth of their team members and the overall organization. The smartest person in the room is not the one who talks the most, but the one who asks the best questions.

> The smartest person in the room is not the one who talks the most, but the one who asks the best questions.

In other cases, a company can identify its unique .1% by exploiting a gap in the marketplace that it is in a particularly advantageous position to fill. My firm helps businesses spot trends, identify gaps, connect insights, and tap opportunities that will dramatically differentiate their brand in their industry. Our goal is to help them identify new core competencies, products, services, and processes so they can leverage what their competitors cannot duplicate in a short period of time. We also help our clients find a path to advance their category by identifying disruptive approaches to capitalize on market channels and outdated value chains aligned with the changing needs of end users.

The first challenge, of course, is to find the unique aspect of your business's DNA. You must force yourself to take time off from managing day-to-day urgent tasks and focus on the bigger picture. Once you identify your unique .1%, align your company's vision to it and develop the operational structure to exploit it. To fully capitalize on the opportunity it presents, you may need to change processes, hire people with special skills, and communicate more powerfully. We'll talk about how to leverage your .1% in succeeding chapters.

The Best Buy Story

Practically every night, I awaken to that damn flashing "12:00" on my DVR. Why do I continue to put up with that incessant flashing? The answer is because I am a technologically challenged Baby Boomer, and I can't figure out how the heck to set the clock on this piece of "high tech" equipment. As a result, I've been putting up with that annoying flashing for several years.

I'm confessing my ineptness with technology to highlight the wisdom of Best Buy's marketing strategy, which is built around the core uniqueness of filling this exact gap. We Boomers have the highest disposable income for spending on things like cool technological innovations, but we also happen to be the least savvy generation when it comes to technology. Best Buy's successful

29

exploitation of this gap between "ability to buy" and "ability to use" provides a good illustration of how to identify and leverage your unique .1%.

Best Buy's competitors have primarily competed on price. Take Circuit City, for example. It was more interested in getting customers to buy a product (any product) than in helping customers understand which products were right for their needs. Because many of Circuit City's salespeople were not well trained (or even very passionate) about innovation and technology, and because they weren't particularly inquisitive about what kind of experience customers wanted with the various types of equipment, sales conversations usually drifted to the lowest common denominator: price. Over time, Circuit City came to rely on discounted prices as its primary marketing and sales approach. This strategy eventually put them out of business.

Best Buy's employees, on the other hand, truly love technology. They live it and breathe it. Because of the company's excellent training, they understand the products they sell, and they enjoy talking with customers about them...a lot! In a sales situation, they ask customers relevant questions about how they would like to *experience the technology* in their home. They readily compare different options for customers, openly share consumer reports with them, and make recommendations based upon their particular needs and goals. This more consultative and less persuasive sales approach actually results in greater customer loyalty and more profitable purchases.

Best Buy knows that Boomers and Gen-Xers have the money to buy technology, but that they often lack the confidence to install or even use it. With this realization, the company built a whole new business model around educating and enabling customers and successfully installing and servicing the products they purchase. Ultimately, Best Buy installs something more important than products: it installs confidence. Because the company has removed the "intimidation factor," Boomers and Gen-Xers who may not have the technical knowledge to even set the clock on a piece of equipment feel very comfortable shopping and spending money at its stores.

For many years Best Buy has clearly proclaimed its unique .1% in the following value proposition:

We Make Technology Deliver on Its Promises
Accessibility • Selection • Price • Service

The company backed up this promise by acquiring the Geek Squad, which provides installation and technology training services to its customers. Although separate financials for Geek Squad are not released to the public, analysts have estimated that this segment of the business generates a gross profit margin of 40% to 50% on annual revenues in excess of $2 billion (about 4% of Best Buy's total revenues of approximately $50 billion).

When I shop at Best Buy, I never feel as if the sales people are pushing a product on me simply to boost their sales commission. Because they always seem to be steering me toward the product that best fits my needs, I feel more comfortable and in control of the selection process. The conversation naturally focuses less on price and more on the product's features and benefits that will fulfill my individual needs. For consumers like me, the major consideration isn't price. We primarily want to be confident that we are getting what we need. Best Buy provides this confidence. That's why it has higher revenue-per-sale and profit-per-sale than Circuit City ever had, and that's why it's still in business and Circuit City is not.

Best Buy recently changed its value proposition to "Expert Service. Unbeatable Price." This new brand promise continues to leverage the company's particular expertise and knowledge, while also promoting its competitive pricing. However, I think Best Buy would have been wiser to adopt a value proposition that doesn't focus on price. For example, "Expert Service. Unbeatable Value." would communicate that the company helps consumers find the right solution at the right price, regardless of their budget.

There is much to learn from this story, no matter what product or service your company sells. First, you must have a vision that specifically anchors your business and serves as a point of alignment for the expected actions of your team. You must stand for something, and your people must know what that is. If you fail to properly train your salespeople and provide them with the right guidance and tools, they will tend to sell what they are most comfortable with. When trying to close the deal on a product they don't understand, they will ultimately rely on the lowest common denominator: price. Focusing on price dramatically limits the profit opportunity per transaction for the company, and it limits the salesperson's ability to provide customers with the best product for their desired outcome.

Customers behave similarly. If they don't understand what makes you different, and they have limited confidence in what the salesperson is selling (or in what the brand is promising), they too will revert to the lowest common denominator to compare products or companies. That is, they will make their purchasing decision primarily based on price. This is exactly the type of interaction that took place between Circuit City and its customers.

From the Best Buy story, you may now have a better appreciation for the value of finding and leveraging your unique .1%. Your .1% must not only add value to your business, but even more importantly, it must be relevant and add value to your customers' desired outcome. For Best Buy, this uniqueness created a differentiated approach that drove its business results up and its major competitor out of the market.

Incidentally, as I write this book, the Circuit City brand is experiencing a resurrection of sorts. Between 2008 and 2015, the brand was essentially irrelevant. Recently, retail veterans Ronny Shmoel and Albert Liniado purchased the Circuit City name, and over the next five years they plan to open 5,000 to 10,000 stores. Learning from the mistakes of the former Circuit City, the new company's strategy will focus on service instead of on price. Mirroring the Radio Shack model, the stores will be smaller (2,000 to 4,000 square feet), the merchandise will be targeted to Millennials, and the sales staffs will be highly trained.

Performance in the Game and in the Stock Market

Nike, the very successful marketer of athletic shoes and apparel, provides us with another positive example of how to find and leverage your unique .1% throughout your business. Founded in 1964 and originally known as Blue Ribbon Sports (BRS), the company originally operated as a distributor for Japanese shoemaker Onitsuka (now ASICS). Initially, the company conducted most of its sales out of the trunk of one of the owners' cars at prominent track meets on the West Coast. In 1971, as the company started to gain momentum and recognition, it became evident that it needed to develop a strong brand. The company transitioned to Nike (named for the Greek goddess of victory) and created a loyal following based upon strong brand positioning.

For several years, Nike played squarely in the performance athletic category in direct competition with Adidas, Converse, Reebok, and other manufacturers. But then it began to think differently about how to provide value to its customers. Without compromising style, the company shifted its focus  from simply increasing the performance of its *products* to increasing the performance of the *users* of its products. Management made a decision to incorporate more technology into the company's products, with the goal of maximizing the performance level of each and every customer, regardless of skill level.

This strategy became Nike's unique .1%, and it worked! Today Nike is one of the world's largest suppliers of athletic shoes and apparel, with revenues of $30.6 billion and more than 63,000 employees worldwide. In 2014, the brand alone—a valuable intangible asset—was valued at $19 billion, making it the most valuable brand among sports businesses. It's amazing what can happen when a company disrupts the industry's "business as usual" routine and intentionally begins thinking differently about the *possibility* of delivering something beyond a mere product.

Quite a Performance!

Cirque du Soleil provides us with another example of the power of thinking differently. When Guy Laliberté and Gilles Ste-Croix, two Canadian street performers, founded the company in 1984, few would have predicted financial success. Although circuses had a long history as a source of exciting, colorful, and fun entertainment for families, they had in recent years become mundane and much less popular. And due to the high costs of moving enormous outdoor productions from city to city and satisfying the growing demands of animal rights activist groups, they had become much less profitable. The category was ripe for either

> De-maturing a market involves rethinking and repositioning a mature market at the end of its life cycle to create the beginning of a new life cycle.

a continued decline or a major "de-maturing." De-maturing a market involves rethinking and repositioning a mature market at the end of its life cycle to create the beginning of a new life cycle.

These two entrepreneurs knew that if they were to succeed, they would have to think differently. Instead of focusing on traditional circus acts for children and adults who might pay an average of $85 per family, they decided to provide refined entertainment experiences for upscale adults who would pay $175 per ticket. With the help of Franco Dragone, the Italian-Belgian theater director, they created dreamlike narratives performed by world-class acrobats and dancers, with state-of-the-art lighting and sophisticated music appropriate for the ages of their target audience. These performances, which Dragone referred to as avant-garde acrobatics, were enormously popular right out of the gate. I have attended several shows personally, and none have disappointed. Nor have I ever heard anyone leaving a show complain about the price of admission. As we saw with Best Buy, and as is true of almost every company in any industry, *it's about the experience, not the price.*

On the surface, Cirque du Soleil and other traditional circuses share 99.9% identical DNA. Both have stirring music, elaborate lighting, thrilling acts, and daredevil performers. But Cirque du

Soleil took a .1% departure from the norm, which turned out to be wildly successful in creating demand. Today, Cirque du Soleil has more than 4,000 employees from approximately 40 countries presenting shows in more than 300 cities around the world.[1] By eliminating animal acts and quadrupling ticket prices, it has also become highly profitable. The company boasts annual revenues of nearly $1 billion and profits of $250 million. In 2017, the organization acquired New York-based Blue Man Productions, a global live entertainment company best known for the award-winning Blue Man Group show. The strategic move was another example of how Cirque du Soleil aims to differentiate itself as a performance outlet. The merger greatly extends Cirque's consumer and geographic reach, adding six resident productions to their portfolio established across the United States and Germany and even into Asia. This is an example of how thinking differently can create not only a higher profit stream, but a new high-energy, high-thrill category within the high-end entertainment industry!

If you want to dramatically enhance your business's performance and financial results, you and your team must learn to think from a different perspective. To ensure success:

1. Set your company apart by identifying the unique .1% of your business's DNA that no one else can claim,

2. Embed that unique DNA into your brand,

3. Embrace it in a way that drives market leadership,

4. Craft your strategy around it,

1   W. Chan Kim and Renee Mauborgne, *Blue Ocean Straegy: How to Create Uncontested Market Space and Make Competition Irrelevant,* 2015 (Harvard Business Review Press, Expanded Edition)

5. Use it as a platform for growth,

6. Lead from it to empower your employees,

7. Filter through it to define what is critical to success,

8. Communicate it to engage your customers, and

9. Quantify it to measure your progress.

In subsequent chapters, we'll talk about how doing these things differently will produce extraordinary business results.

2

LIVING YOUR PROMISE

Your brand is the single most important
investment you can make in your business.
—Steve Forbes

The *Oxford American Dictionary* defines a brand as a "type of product manufactured by a particular company under a particular name." But this definition merely addresses the functional aspect of the word, not its true comprehensive meaning from a business standpoint. So, what exactly is a brand, and why is it so important? How can branding impact your business's success?

A brand is much more than a mere logo you stamp on your stationery, business cards, marketing materials, and products. It's the ultimate reflection of your company to the external market, and it's a vital guide to your internal team. To better understand the breadth of meaning and importance of the word, let's take a brief look at its entomological evolution.

It appears that the word brand was first used around 1400 A.D., when it meant torch. A torch provides light, and today like a torch, your brand should light the way. It should help guide you on your path to your ultimate destination, and it should illuminate your company and its products, so the world can see them clearly. And just as the fire of a torch also gives off heat that provides warmth and comfort to those interacting with it, your brand should attract attention, generate excitement, and engender positive and comforting feelings from those who come in contact with it. You need to be mindful, however, that just as a torch can cause damage if used carelessly, your brand can do damage to your company if not properly handled.

Around 1550 A.D., the word brand became an alternative word for sword. A sword is an instrument of battle with a sharp point and two sharp edges. Like a sword, you should use the point (the finely tuned message) and the sharp edges (the delivery) of your brand promise to cut through the clutter of the marketplace. Just as swords can be used offensively and defensively, you should use your brand both to defend your position in the marketplace and to attack competitors who try to undermine it. In the 14th century, swords were individually customized for their owners. Your brand should provide relevant value to each segment of your target market. And finally, just as a sword's two sharp edges can cut both ways, you must be careful about how you employ your brand, because improper use can harm your business.

In the early 1800s, people began defining a brand as a hot iron that ranchers use to burn a distinguishing mark into the hide of livestock, to signal ownership. Today, bidders at cattle auctions know from experience which ranchers raise their cattle with the best grazing conditions and the best care, and they are willing to pay premium prices for cattle bearing these ranchers' brands. In a similar way, your brand embodies your authentic brand promise. It identifies the value that your company and your company's products will provide. Just as a cattle brand differentiates one owner's livestock from another's, your company's uniquely owned brand differentiates your solutions from your competitors'.

Your brand is your most valuable possession. It conveys your promise to your customers and to the world. Safeguard, nurture, and enhance the value of your brand by keeping your promise and living up to your commitments.

I Promise...

Your promise is an emotional assurance that you will do what you say. How would you feel if someone broke any one of the following promises to you:

I promise to be there at 10:00 a.m. to help you move your furniture.
I promise to always tell you the truth.
I promise to be true to you in good times and in bad, in sickness and in health.

Failure to keep a promise can cause deep disappointment and emotional disconnection. In marketing terms, your brand is your promise. It tells people what they can expect when interacting with your company, your products, and your employees. It is the experience you create in these interactions. People will feel disappointed and even abandoned if your brand lets them down.

When you continually fulfill your promise, your brand can be your most powerful marketing and sales tool. A strong brand serves as your ambassador throughout the industry, creating connection and confidence. But failing to keep your brand promise can hurt people's trust in your company. It will erode loyalty and positive mind share, causing your company considerable harm and negative momentum. You can also damage your brand simply by presenting it inconsistently at the various touch points where you interact with your existing and potential customers.

In the home improvement industry, for example, consumers making a major purchase ($2,000 or more) will typically interact at five touch points before they make a final decision. These interactions may occur through such channels as:

- Dealer showrooms

- Big-box retail stores

- The manufacturer's website

- Social media

- Independent reviews

- Specialty-content websites (e.g., Houzz)

- Word of mouth of friends and neighbors

- Professional contractors or builders

- Company employees

- Company branding and marketing efforts

If any of these touch points represent your brand inconsistently by communicating conflicting stories or by misrepresenting what you actually offer, buyers will become confused. Confusion is more than a nuisance. It can cause customers to lose confidence in your company and your products, resulting in brand abandonment, or the purchase altogether, loss of loyalty, and possibly a tarnished long-term reputation.

Strengthening Your Brand

The role of a brand is to deliver a strong and consistent promise that creates customer loyalty. Loyal customers will believe so strongly in your brand and be so emotionally connected to it that an increase in price of 5%, 10%, or even 20% will not necessarily deter them from continuing to do business with you. They will come back to purchase from your company time and time again, even if your relationship hits some speed bumps along the way.

Research by Mike Johnston at The Chartered Institute of Marketing has shown that acquiring a new customer can cost up to 30 times as much as retaining an existing one. It naturally follows, then, that customer loyalty increases company profitability. All other things being equal, a company will generate considerably higher profits by selling repeatedly to a few customers than by selling the same quantity of product to many newly acquired customers.

[

…acquiring a new customer can cost up to 30 times as much as retaining an existing one.

]

So, what makes a strong brand, and how can you strengthen yours? Not necessarily by spending lots of money. Many large companies with sizable promotional budgets have weak brands. A powerful brand is one that makes a strong, authentic emotional connection to the audiences it is meant to influence. Your brand derives its strength from your faithfulness in living your brand promise in all that you do. A strong brand lights the path and will accurately represent your company and its products externally to your customers, suppliers, and the community, while at the same time providing guidance and focus internally for your employees.

To obtain this higher level of interaction, your brand needs to be more than merely functional. It must be relevant to people's needs, and it must offer something special. In other words, it must embody the unique .1% of your company's DNA that differentiates your business from the competition. True differentiation increases business equity.

Brand equity is about creating incremental value, first for your customers and consequently for your company. If you rely primarily on functional attributes rather than emotional connections to establish your brand equity, price will become your ultimate sales tool. When price is the primary differentiator of your brand, profitability is the inevitable casualty.

Once you have established a robust brand, you must keep it strong by truly living your brand promise. At all touch points, consistently say what you do, and in all your interactions, faithfully do what you say. In the remainder of this chapter and throughout this book, we'll take a look at some companies that did—or did not do—a good job of keeping their brand promise.

Everything *Plus* the Kitchen Sink

Kohler is an example of a strong brand in the building materials and home improvement industries. Like other strong brands, it evolved over a period of many years, adapting to the changing environments and taking advantage of what I call "happy accidents of innovation."

The Kohler brand got its start in 1873, when John Michael Kohler, an Australian immigrant and businessman, purchased a foundry in rural Wisconsin that produced a variety of steel and cast-iron farm implements. One day in the early 1880s, Kohler engineers took a cast-iron trough used for feeding livestock, heated it to 177 degrees Fahrenheit, and sprinkled enamel powder over it. The glossy, smooth, and durable finish this process produced so impressed Kohler that he placed a picture of the enamel trough in the company's catalog that year with the caption, "A horse trough/hog scalder...and when finished with four legs, will serve as a bathtub." Ever since that day, Kohler has been a market leader in the plumbing category.

Once it committed to market leadership in this new category, the Kohler Company kept innovating relevant products aligned with trends in the industry. For example, in 1926 it announced the "Kohler electric sink," the forerunner to the modern dishwasher. Also, noticing the consumer trend toward more colorful products in everything from clothes to automobiles to home furnishings, Kohler started offering cast-iron tubs and china plumbing products (sinks and toilets) in exact matching pastel colors, initiating the market trend of coordinated, design-centric bathrooms. The influence of the company's use of softer pastel colors in the home created trends that some say even impacted the color offerings of automobiles.

Kohler continued to differentiate its brand by introducing bolder colors and more advanced designs. These innovations so powerfully influenced the company's brand that in 1967 Kohler's marketing team came up with the tagline, "The Bold Look of Kohler." Since then, Kohler has leveraged the word "bold" to encompass its state-of-the-art technological innovations, dramatic styles and finishes, and even support programs for dealers and retailers. The company's dedication to design innovation has engendered intense brand loyalty. A 2007 television commercial of a husband and wife talking to a prestigious architect about the design of their new home perfectly captured this brand image. Placing a Kohler faucet on a barren table, the wife says to the architect, "Design a house around this (faucet)."

A brand isn't a rubber stamp you can put on any product to automatically ensure success. However, a company can leverage a strong brand across multiple industries if its brand promise and its products are relevant to each category's needs. Kohler is an example of a company that has successfully made its brand relevant in the power, interiors, and hospitality industries. Of course, to be successful over the long term, the company must faithfully fulfill its unique brand promise to the audiences within each of these industries.

Protecting Your Brand

We saw in Chapter 1 how Best Buy and Cirque du Soleil built successful businesses by clearly identifying their unique .1% and building their brand and customer experience around it. Their brands remain strong because they live their brand promise consistently at every touch point, and they continually look for ways to advance their category through strong and innovative leadership.

But even the strongest brands can falter at times. Why is this? A few of the most common reasons are: myopic planning, off-target innovation, inwardly focused product development, lack of relevance to the target audience, misaligned organizational goals, and unfulfilled promises. Nike provides us with an example of how a brand can lose its way, in spite of a company's solid track record of brand faithfulness.

In the last chapter, we talked about how Nike differentiated itself by transitioning from merely selling on-trend, high-performance sports gear to selling on-trend sports gear that would enable individual users to perform at their highest level. But in 1995, eyeing the expanding market in hockey and inline skates, Nike departed from this brand promise when it purchased Canstar Sports Inc. for $395 million. Canstar was the parent company of Bauer, the leading manufacturer in the hockey skate category. Co-branding a line of products for the first time in its history, Nike intended to leverage *Nike Bauer* into a premier brand in the developing hockey category.

The concept wasn't necessarily bad, but Nike was inexperienced in the hockey segment of the market and obviously overconfident that its brand could be relevant anywhere. The hockey skates and apparel the company developed, although stylish, were not up to the performance standards true hockey players expected. Breaking its brand promise of offering high-performance hockey products and defaulting on the historical performance expectations of the Bauer brand caused Nike to lose credibility and share in this category.

After many challenging years of trying to make the co-branding work, Nike in 2008 reportedly sold its Bauer assets to Quebec-based Roustan Inc. and U.S.-based private equity firm Kohlberg & Co. for $200 million (a $195 million reduction from the purchase price). The new owners immediately changed the company's name back to Bauer, and over time it reclaimed its premier position in the hockey category with the brand promise of "providing hockey players with the cutting edge products that give them a competitive edge and undeniable confidence." Today, this commitment to quality and innovation has once again made Bauer the most recognized and sought after name in hockey.

More recently, I noticed that Nike's brand seems to be slipping in another way. I recently took my daughter into a Nike store in San Francisco, intending to show her an upscale, exciting place to shop, because that's what I had previously experienced at Nike stores in Chicago and New York City. When we entered the store, however, we both were totally underwhelmed. Instead of the novel brand "experience" I had expected, the store was simply a showcase for products.

The good news is that Nike can easily remedy this situation. The company continues to own more than 60% of the U.S. athletic shoe market, and its brand is still thriving and relevant. Nike CEO Mark Parker, whom *Fortune* magazine named 2015 Businessperson of the Year, has promised to boost the company's annual sales to $50 billion by 2020.

Nevertheless, Nike cannot afford to coast. Under Armour, one of its chief influential competitors, has done an outstanding job of aggressively creating an original brand and associated experiences. For instance, it has secured athletic program partnerships from top universities such as Notre Dame, UCLA, and Wisconsin. As other brands in this category have apparently become a little more complacent, Under Armour has grown from a manufacturer and marketer of undergarments to a major player in the full gamut of athletic apparel, including shoes. According to *Retail Dive*, Under Armour forecasts growth of 25% annually, closing in on revenues of nearly $5 billion. This illustrates the power and tenacity of startups and the need for vigilance in protecting your brand and the space where you company plays.

Netflix made a marketing error similar to Nike's when it violated its brand promise of entertainment accessibility by trying to initiate a rather complex and costly new subscription model for its customers. Fortunately, the company basically returned to its previous approach before it lost too many subscribers. Netflix is highly respected for its many disruptive innovations in the entertainment industry, so this departure from its brand promise was merely a speed bump that is now viewable only in the rearview mirror.

Penney Foolish

The JCPenney story gives us another prime example of what happens when a business decides to dramatically shift its business model and depart from its brand promise. In this case the company focused on the shiny new penny instead of on its valuable JCPenney heritage and brand.

Although never a disruptor, JCPenney had over the years maintained its reputation as one of the nation's most successful retailers. It had always stayed true to its brand promise of providing good value and choice to its key customers, which traditionally were women aged 40 to 60 in the middle-income demographics. The company had very high brand loyalty with this core audience, and its performance was at or above retail market benchmarks. Then JCPenney made a monumental branding (and business) mistake.

In 2012, the JCPenney board decided to reinvent the company and refresh its brand to appeal to today's younger, trendier consumers. To execute this transformation, they hired as the company's new CEO a former Apple executive who had been largely responsible for the success of Apple's retail stores. The prospect of updating JCPenney's brand image and stores excited the company's board of directors, and the board in turn excited investors. After all, change is good, isn't it?

Under the leadership of the new CEO, JCPenney spent considerable time and an estimated $50 million developing a trendy new brand approach designed to appeal primarily to Millennials, its newly chosen target audience. Because these younger consumers preferred contemporary interactions, the company worked with a new branding agency at breakneck speed to come up with a fresh approach catering to this new audience.

One of the first decisions was to change the company's name from JCPenney to JCP. The next steps were to redesign the stores, change the apparel brands and selection, and eliminate merchandise coupons and discounts. Unfortunately, these changes caused the company's traditional core audience (their brand ambassadors) to desert the brand in droves. To make matters worse, the Millennials who were supposed to be the new target market had no emotional connection to the brand, and they had far less disposable income to spend than the original core audience. Also, these new customers preferred to shop online and JCPenney had created a poor digital experience.

What went wrong? The major problem was that JCPenney abandoned its unique brand promise to its core audience. There's nothing wrong with going after additional audiences, as long as you remain true to your brand promise to your existing brand champions, the core audience that has traditionally paid your bills and sounded your praise. This core audience liked coupons and special sales. They shopped and walked the stores in a particular way, and these changes, which seemed to come out of nowhere, made them feel uncomfortable. The new JCP violated a cardinal rule of marketing: Never make your brand ambassadors feel uncomfortable with your brand.

> ...a cardinal rule of marketing: Never make your brand ambassadors feel uncomfortable with your brand.

JCPenney's other problem was brand inconsistency. On one hand, the company was running cool, energetic advertising and social media campaigns targeting the new class of consumers. But when buyers came into a store, they saw a hodgepodge of styles and partly transitioned departments with many new brands not yet in stock. The in-store experience did not live up to anything like the digital brand experience. The confusion resulting from this inconsistency caused this new audience of Millennials to abandon the JCP brand before the new store and brand approach even had a chance to develop loyalty. And the company's historical core customers abandoned JCP because the new brand and in-store approach wasn't designed to appeal to them.

To JCPenney's credit, the board quickly corrected this misstep, as soon as it fully realized the costly disconnect it had created. The board changed the company's name back to JCPenney, terminated the new CEO, and rehired the previous CEO, Mike Ullman. He immediately bought TV time and personally visited with the company's core audience in their living rooms. "We apologize for our mistake," he said. "Please come back to the JCPenney you have known and supported."

The company delivered this sincere and humble "apology ad" via TV and social media, and it gave away $50 gift cards for feedback on what they were doing right and wrong. The message connected with the intended core audience and produced the desired results. As the company began delivering on its original promise, the value of the company's shares immediately increased 2.9% and kept rising.

In August 2015, Ullman handed CEO responsibilities over to Marvin Ellison, who started his career as a security guard at Target and earned his retailing spurs by helping to engineer a turnaround at Home Depot. In a recent cover story titled "Saving Penneys," *Fortune* magazine[2] detailed how Ellison is continuing the work of righting the JCPenney ship through a series of common-sense retailing and operational improvements, increased reliance on data, and an engaged management style evidenced by more than 60 employee town hall meetings and visiting more than 100 stores to engage directly with employees in his first five months on the job. Although the company's performance is trending upward, some retail industry experts doubt that it will ever regain its former luster, especially like all retailers trying to forecast the impact Amazon will have on their category. But as JCPenney seeks to balance serving its core customers and re-reinventing itself, one can be certain that it will never again break its brand promise.

Promises are powerful. Getting all your employees (and sometimes other stakeholders and the board of directors) to buy into and

---

2   *Fortune* magazine, Nov. 12, 2015, 76

consistently deliver on your brand promise is critical to your business's success. As we will discuss in the next chapter, your brand promise is your platform for market leadership. If you happen to temporarily get derailed from keeping it (and everyone does at some point), exercise decisive leadership to quickly get your organization back on track. The examples in this chapter illustrate that missteps can be costly, especially if they drag on, but timely corrective action can keep them from being fatal.

3

REDEFINING MARKET LEADERSHIP

The only way to control change is to lead it.
 —Theodore Roosevelt

When I ask executives who the leader is in their market, the vast majority will name the company with the greatest percentage of market share. But I think this myopic definition of market leadership can undermine the very leadership you want to promote. It has the potential to impair your business decision-making and handcuff your team.

Other executives say the market leader is the company that exercises the greatest influence over the market. This definition also misses the mark. The ability to influence price shifts, capacity constraints, or otherwise impact the marketplace doesn't make a company a market leader. It merely indicates that the company has the capacity, clout, or propensity to exert influence.

Influencing isn't necessarily leading. Would you call a company that uses its influence to maintain the status quo in a market a legitimate market leader? What about a company that negatively influences a market by squashing codes or regulations for its own benefit, or a company that influences a market by using price as a weapon to eliminate a competitor? And how about a business that buys an innovative competitor only to shut it down, so as to manage innovation and capacity? These may be shrewd business decisions in certain cases, but they are not the actions of a market leader. These companies are solely focused on optimizing their individual results for a period of time, not on advancing the whole industry in a sustainable fashion. I believe a true market leader can both deliver outstanding business results *and* advance the categories in which it plays.

True Market Leadership

A true market leader is a company that actively advances a product category, a market, and—ideally—an entire industry. Market leadership is about impacting the market to help it grow and prosper. It's about advancement, not merely influence or control.

> A true market leader is a company that actively advances a product category, a market, and—ideally—an entire industry.

The word "advance" denotes a positive forward direction. Advancement requires vision, commitment, and involvement. Companies with a dominant market share may *influence* a market by introducing new products or leading price increases, but only companies that truly understand the industry and embed themselves in the industry's success through good times and bad can *advance* the market. Real market leaders live within the fray. They exhibit a committed, persevering, and involved leadership that almost always results in success. When necessary, they even have the courage to disrupt their own businesses. "Anyone can hold the helm when the sea is calm," said the Latin writer Publilius Syrus. And to that I would add, but only true leaders embrace the helm in the storm.

Smaller players or new entrants into a category will often advance a market more than larger, more established companies. Some companies that have the largest share in their category are not focused on taking the industry in any new or positive direction. They're merely making products as efficiently as they can, and 75% to 85% of these products are merely commodities. They're constantly looking for ways to reduce material costs, increase efficiencies, and increase their market share, so they can fill their production lines and spread their investment in manufacturing plant and equipment over a larger volume. It's as if they are playing a game of chess with share and price to maximize shareholder value. Optimizing short-term results for your shareholders is important, but don't confuse it with industry leadership.

I have observed over and over that even a relatively small company, given sufficient time, can advance a category or even an entire industry. Some companies may rank third or fourth in market share position in their industry, or they may be a relatively new upstart company and yet, they can play a more important role in advancing and innovating the category than the company with the most share, profit dollars, and the most manufacturing assets.

Disruption has transformed many product categories—and even industries—over the last 20 years. However, disruption is now happening with greater momentum and frequency. It's the new normal, barreling toward your business. If you are not proactively participating or leading disruptive change, it will work against you.

Hitting the Deck to Advance Outdoor Living

Inventor and entrepreneur Roger Wittenberg launched the innovation to replace wood in 1988 when he combined sawdust and plastic bags to create long-lasting and environmentally friendly park benches. By the early 1990s, he had big plans for this new technology platform, as well as a barn full of recycled plastic. In 1996, he sold the technology to Mobil Chemical Co., and later that same year Mobile sold the technology to a newly formed business, Trex Company LLC. Trex then proceeded to create a new category of wood-alternative decking, which offered significant maintenance advantages to millions of homeowners and contractors who installed decks each year.

Because of the success of Trex's leadership, other composite (wood-alternative) decking competitors entered the market, which helped to create more awareness and credibility for the category. Because of this momentum, composite decks have grown rapidly in popularity, now accounting for more than a third of newly installed decks. Trex, the decking category brand leader, communicates its brand promise with the slogan, "Outdoor living, elevated." In its marketing materials, the company boasts that it manufactures its products from 95% recycled plastic bags, wood scraps, and other recycled materials, and that it has never cut down a tree.

History has shown us time and again that market leaders must continue to be aggressive in order to maintain their position. As has been the case with numerous other categories, new companies are entering the decking category on differentiated brand promises and innovative approaches that leverage safety, durability, and distinctive appearance. They are continuing to advance the category by creating new technology platforms that evolve in response to the industry's gaps and unmet needs. To address these competitive influences, Trex continues to exercise market leadership in the outdoor living category by extending its brand and product offerings to adjacent categories like lighting and furniture. In future years, it will be interesting to see how these new disruptor companies advance and impact the category.

Hard Work and High Energy

Market leadership demands hard work, perseverance, and an open mind. To advance a category, you must focus your eyes on your goals while alertly looking for gaps to fill and trends to leverage. For example, which of these proclamations do you think your employees would rather hear in your next "town hall meeting"?

- *We will continue to aggressively sell the most products in our industry, making every effort to maintain our leadership share position, while taking every precaution to keep our competitors from catching us.*

- *We will powerfully leverage the talents and dedication of our team by thinking differently and redefining what is possible, with the goal of continually advancing the category and our customers' success, so as to ultimately maximize our own success.*

Both statements can be a good path for your business and a valid focus for your team. However, the second proclamation is more exciting and engaging. Customers and employees are attracted to action-oriented organizations that are continually evolving because of their commitment to a strong vision, innovation, and empowerment. That's also the type of company new employee recruits want to join, and it's the type of company customers and suppliers want to partner with.

I watch sports constantly to see how coaches lead, how individual players take accountability, and how teams perform. So, permit me to use a sports analogy to further illustrate my point. Imagine you are the new, highly rated quarterback on a team, and you are just about to get your chance to shine for the season. But before the kickoff, the coach comes over to you and whispers something in your ear. Which of the following two pep talks would you rather hear?

• I want you to just manage the game. Don't overthink this. Don't put the team in a risky situation where we might lose.

• You have a great team around you. I know you are well prepared, and I trust that you have the leadership to execute our vision and take advantage of the different opportunities that will come your way during the game. Be smart, bold, and confident. Now, go out there and lead this team to victory!

Unfortunately, the majority of companies with the biggest market share in an industry are like the first example above. Mistakenly, they think they can "circle the wagons," play conservatively, and still maintain their leadership position. They are like a sports team that builds up a lead and then starts playing cautiously to try to protect it. But in business, as in sports, playing "not to lose" instead of "to win" usually backfires. It typically results in a harvest approach (like the upcoming Kodak example in which the company insisted on protecting their film share until the film category virtually went away), not a growth approach.

Sports teams that play "not to lose" near the end of the game usually end up losing contests they should have won. When what could have been an outstanding season turns into a subpar one, fans are not happy, team members become disengaged, and the coaching staff (the leadership team) usually pays the price. When you as a leader lose your vision, your team loses focus on the game plan, and your business loses out on achieving its desired business results.

Companies that simply try to protect their market share may continue to think of themselves as leaders, and for a period of time other companies in the industry may regard them as such. But ultimately, they will lose momentum, market share, connection to the industry, leverage, and respect. The market no longer waits eagerly for the company's next exciting innovation, because customers have learned that there won't be one. When this happens, the company's leadership impact and business results can significantly decline. True market leaders view challenges, gaps, and speed bumps as opportunities to redefine and evolve the game plan so it more effectively achieves the desired outcome.

The Leader's Trap

Why do companies with the biggest share of a market so often fail to exercise true market leadership? At one time, they must have been consciously seeking to advance the market by aggressively taking advantage of unusual, growth-oriented opportunities. Otherwise, they wouldn't have become so large. So, what caused them to alter their mindset and actions?

Numerous business books and articles have addressed this question, and there seems to be general agreement about the answer. In fact, the syndrome that causes companies with majority market share to lose their moxie is so common that it even has a name. It's called "the leader's trap."

Companies fall into the *leader's trap* when they become so afraid of losing their dominant position within an industry that they prioritize market stability over market leadership. Out of fear of making a mistake that will cause them to lose market share or price, they become excessively cautious. This timidity ultimately handicaps the company's leadership team, employees, and suppliers. It even eventually flows out to its customers.

> Companies fall into the *leader's trap* when they become so afraid of losing their dominant position within an industry that they prioritize market stability over market leadership.

At a fundamental level, the cause of the leader's trap is *fear of change.* Change can sometimes result in disruption, and disruption is inconvenient and uncomfortable. In fact, it can feel (and sometimes can actually be) life-threatening to an organization. But change and disruption are prerequisites for advancement. They're the standard currency for creating innovative products and bold new ideas. Very little meaningful innovation takes place without some level of disruption and discomfort within an industry, a category, or a company.

Disruption is most threatening to companies with the largest market share because these companies have the most invested in their current products, pricing structures, distribution channels, technologies, plant assets, inventory, and processes. Disruptive decisions can necessitate uncomfortable personnel changes, product alterations, write-offs of inventory and assets, adjustments in marketing and distribution approaches, and shifts in business and production processes across multiple regions and distribution channels.

Because companies with large market share usually have the most to lose from disruptions, they are more likely to try to "play it safe." Consciously or unconsciously, they fall into the leader's trap by choosing to be maintainers rather than leaders. That's why some of the strongest advancements come not from market share leaders, but from smaller companies within or even outside of a category. These companies are like the "Cinderella teams" in the NCAA "March Madness" basketball tournament. They figure they have less to lose than the high-profile teams, so they are more willing to stretch boundaries and shake things up.

In the building-material industry, for example, some of the major product disruptions have included vinyl siding (versus aluminum), composite doors (versus wood), composite decks (versus wood), engineered wood (versus plywood), spray foam insulation (versus fiberglass), and tankless water heaters (versus tank water heaters). Interestingly, none of these disruptions came from the market share leaders. Why? Because the share leaders were busy protecting their space, their products, their profits, and their investments in their manufacturing assets.

Over the long term, the ultimate costs you must pay to merely maintain can far exceed the costs of leading. Eastman Kodak Company is a case in point. At one time, Kodak was the undisputed leader in the photographic film category. As the market-share leader, it also had the biggest investment in existing technologies.

When digital processing began to replace film in the late 1990s, Kodak was very slow to react. Although it had invested in innovation and had actually developed the very first digital camera in 1975, it had quickly eliminated the product out of fear it would lead to cannibalization of the company's photographic film business. Kodak fell into the leader's trap by attempting to protect its existing share. Eventually, its competitors disrupted the industry with digital technology and cannibalized dramatic amounts of share from Kodak's once dominant market-share position.

In January 2012, the company filed for Chapter 11 bankruptcy protection.[3] It continues in business making niche products, but today its $1.7 billion in annual sales pales in comparison with its $19 billion in revenues in 1990, when consumer film was king. The 6,000 employees the company has worldwide today are a fraction of the 145,000 it had when it was a share leader.

The detrimental effects of the leader's trap can permeate the culture of an organization. When employees notice that the company is more interested in merely maintaining its position and protecting the cash cow than in pursuing new opportunities, they lose their enthusiasm, commitment, competitive edge, innovative momentum, and entrepreneurial spirit. Excessive conservatism in problem-solving breeds an environment of complacency. People become

---

3   In September 2013, Kodak emerged from bankruptcy. The company now primarily provides packaging, functional printing, graphic communications and professional services for businesses around the world.

apprehensive about pushing new ideas. Instead of working with purpose, they merely go through the motions. They fill their days with routine tasks while ignoring new trends or the critical issues that would truly move the company forward. This is playing "not to lose" at its finest. And you will lose your best people in this scenario.

Eventually, the effects of this internal stagnation will manifest themselves to the outside world. Customers will feel it, and competitors will swoop in to capitalize on the opportunities the company has passed up or simply overlooked. New competition will enter and redefine the category. The company's brand will lose its luster, customers will drift away, and sales will shrink to a point where the company is equal to or less than the other players in the category, losing all leverage in the industry.

I have witnessed companies with dominant market-share position sit back and play a chess game of balancing volume, profit, and share position. Over a period of ten to 20 years, their share of the market will decline 20 or more points. Fear of losing

> ...if you are going to be cannibalized, cannibalize yourself rather than let someone else take both your business and the credit for advancing the industry.

market share becomes a self-fulfilling prophecy. A prevailing attitude of "protectionism" creates a fertile ground for small competitors to grow at a rapid pace through investments in capacity, technology, and disruptive approaches to the market. I am a true believer that if you are going to be cannibalized, cannibalize yourself rather than let someone else take both your business and the credit for advancing the industry.

An Ongoing Commitment to Disruption

Several large companies like Netflix and Amazon have a history of disrupting themselves. This can be—and has been—successfully accomplished in many industries. Owens Corning, a *Fortune* 1000 company in the building products industry, has historically looked for opportunities to be a disruptor, innovator, and advancer in several categories. In its industry, for example, the company has done an exemplary job of identifying market needs and filling them with innovations connected to its core competency of producing glass fibers in several forms and fashions.

When fiberglass was invented by Owens Corning in the early 1930s, it was initially used in filtration products. But in the late 1930s, a "happy accident of innovation" occurred during experimentation that alerted the company to its application as an insulating material.

The insulation category is essentially about making homes and offices more comfortable, quiet, and energy-efficient. Rather than simply inventing insulation products and pushing them out to market with the hope that they would catch on, Owens Corning worked with the Department of Energy and the Environmental Protection Agency, investing heavily in creating test homes, conducting experiments with thermal-imaging capabilities, and building one of the best acoustical labs in the country. Its products for both the building trade and the do-it-yourself installation market have not only had positive impacts on the environment, but they have forever changed the efficiency and comfort expectations of the construction industry.

Owens Corning continued to innovate by introducing fiberglass technology into other categories of the construction industry and into the home-remodeling market it knew so well. Meanwhile, the company also noticed opportunities in the household bathroom category. In the early 1960s, the iron and enamel bathtubs popular at the time were so heavy that two or three men were required to install them. The enamel also chipped easily  and was extraordinarily expensive to replace. Utilizing its fiberglass technology, Owens Corning created much lighter tubs and showers in a variety of colors and styles. It sold this division in the late 1980s to Sterling Plumbing: Performa, which is now a subsidiary of The Kohler Company.

Continuing the story of innovation, in the early 1970s, the transfer of noise was one of the biggest problems in office buildings and in the home basements that were more frequently being utilized as living spaces. Spotting this need, Owens Corning became a market leader in the ceiling tile category. It developed a fiberglass ceiling tile with strong sound absorption qualities for noise control and a high thermal value, which also reduced heating and air conditioning costs. The company sold this business to Armstrong Industries in the late 1980s.

Also in the 1970s, Owens Corning began to broaden its focus to exterior building issues. At the time, traditional organic roofing shingles were made from asphalt-covered cardboard mat, which deteriorated rather rapidly. Building on their knowledge of fiberglass technology, the company's scientists invented fiberglass-mat roofing shingles that lasted nearly twice as long. Initially, existing shingle manufacturers were unwilling to switch to these new fiberglass mats, so in 1977 Owens Corning bought Frye Roofing Company and led the transition by vertical integration. Because of the company's vision and leadership, the residential roofing market today almost exclusively uses fiberglass shingles, much to the benefit of builders, contractors, and homeowners.

True market leaders also look for opportunities outside of their base industry, as we saw earlier with Kohler. For example, in 1954 Owens Corning partnered with General Motors and Robert Morrison of MFG (a composite parts manufacturer) to create the first molded fiberglass-reinforced plastic body for an automobile—the Corvette. Fiberglass technology opened the door to more creative designs and dramatically better gas mileage. Other manufacturers soon began using it extensively for their automobile bodies and parts. Manufacturers in the airline industry noticed these successes and also began taking advantage of fiberglass technology.

But even Owens Corning has not been immune to cannibalization. Companies from outside the industry have disrupted the home insulation category Owens Corning created by introducing cellulose (paper) insulation, spray foam insulation, and other technologies as alternatives to fiberglass. To date, these competitors have secured only moderate market share, but some would argue that they have advanced the category to a new level of innovation. Only time will tell.

I believe that continual disruption is necessary for the advancement of a category or an industry. Regardless of the source of the disruption, its effects will almost invariably be beneficial. "Competition is like cod liver oil," said Samuel Kaufman. "At first it makes you sick, but then it makes you better." I totally agree. Ultimately, competition is good, because it forces companies to continue to innovate. Society benefits from the new products and the new approaches that result from this new thinking, and companies benefit from high business performance.

Looking to Future Needs

Many forward-looking businesses have demonstrated outstanding market leadership by innovatively filling gaps, solving problems, and even creating trends. One example is 3M, which demonstrates its market leadership by advancing the categories where it plays and even by creating new categories. According to the company's annual report and analysts' reviews, 3M keeps careful track of new product development using its "New Product Vitality Index" (NPVI), which quantifies the percentage of the company's sales that are derived from products introduced in the past five years. The company's NPVI has historically been in the low 30% range (which far exceeds most other corporations), and its longer-term goal is 37%. As a result of its successful policy of innovation, 3M has paid its investors dividends every year since 1916, and for more than 46 consecutive years it has increased them annually.

Apple is another disruptive company that would certainly come to most people's minds. Apple didn't invent the iPhone in response to what people specifically wanted, and it didn't set out to develop the "next cool product." Rather, Steve Jobs envisioned how people would be engaging with each other in the future, and then he led his company to leverage technology to forward-design the connectivity and functionality to match those evolving needs and interactions. Apple continues to innovate and introduce new offerings based on this approach, but as of late, have allowed other companies to drive innovation more quickly.

Companies whose employees sit around the conference room table and try to create products that will optimize what people want *today* will never be highly successful. The same is true of companies that try to develop products based on what has worked in the past. The most successful companies are constantly evolving and disrupting themselves. They look at the gaps and how needs and tastes are trending, and they identify (or create) the unique .1% that fills these gaps and exploits the opportunities they observe. Then they leverage that uniqueness with all their organizational energy.

Unfortunately, true market leaders are somewhat rare. Most companies are content to make only modest improvements from year to year. Preferring comfort to advancement, they have little tolerance for the

> If you want to be a market leader, you must become comfortable with being uncomfortable.

disruption (and the resulting discomfort) required for significant innovation. But true market leaders cannibalize their own products when necessary for advancement, instead of passively protecting their *self-imposed* reality until the competition does the cannibalization for and to them.

If you want to be a market leader, you must become comfortable with being uncomfortable. You need to embrace disruption, not only with your products, but also with how you approach the market. You have to do more than tolerate disruption; you must deliberately seek it out and cultivate it. Encourage some of your more creative and outspoken employees to be catalysts for change in meetings. Consider having outside "disruption consultants" facilitate meetings. Make sure disruption is welcomed throughout your organization. Encourage it at every opportunity. If your company doesn't learn to harness the power of disruption, sooner or later somebody outside of your company will. And then they will use it to disrupt you!

Driving a New Direction

Have you ever stood in the rain and competed with several others for the next available taxi? When one finally stopped and picked you up, did the uncertainty about the cost make you leery of being "taken for a ride"? Did you wonder if the driver would be nice or nasty? When you reached your final destination, did you feel pressured by the driver's impatience as you fumbled for money to pay the fare?

If you've ever had to hail a taxi in a city, these pain points are probably familiar to you. Until recently, most of us figured that taxi services were pretty much the same all over the world, so we resigned ourselves to putting up with the way things were, including U.S. cab companies.

But Travis Kalanick and Garrett Camp, the founders of the highly successful Uber Technologies Inc., took time to think differently. As they looked at this category of the transportation industry, which in the United States includes a massive 6,300 taxicab companies operating approximately 171,000 taxicabs that transport about 1.4 billion passengers annually, they realized it was ripe for disruption.

Kalanick and Camp developed a business model for a transportation service that enables people to travel more easily on their own time. In just a few short years, it has evolved into the largest taxi service in the world. Uber offers a highly flexible, seamless transportation experience to millions of people around the world. It has also opened up thousands of jobs for drivers to work part time on flexible schedules. And because its focus is on redefining the transportation experience, it has evolved its model into partnerships to transport packages, meals, and other high volume purchases.

Uber is successful largely because it's so convenient. You can order an Uber taxi while sitting at your table in a restaurant. Your smart phone will tell you how soon your taxi will arrive, the name of the driver, the exact car, how much you will need to pay, and the rating of your driver—all before the cab comes into view. No more need to stand in the street waving your arms. No more need to walk to the next corner in hopes of getting away from the other taxi-seekers. And no more need to fumble for money at your destination.

This concept seems very simple, but if it's so simple, why didn't any of the 6,300 existing taxicab companies disrupt the industry with it? One answer is that they were preoccupied with the urgent issues of maintaining the status quo in the existing industry. They didn't spend time identifying gaps in the market and developing new insights about customer needs that would dramatically drive business results to a different level and potentially accelerate the growth of the industry.

However, no matter if you operate traditionally or aim to disrupt, every brand has certain responsibilities on how it must conduct itself and the culture it creates. Uber apparently lost their compass on the basics of how to treat employees. This major misstep derailed their business momentum and credibility, both internally and externally.

The Right to Disrupt

You have the right to be the leader in your market, but you must be confident enough to take it. Whether you're number one in market share or number ten, you have a right to disrupt the norm.

You can innovate. You can be the knowledge leader in your industry. You can be the "go-to" company for people in your category who need help solving problems, including

> You have the right to be the leader in your market, but you must be confident enough to take it.

problems they don't even know they have. It's up to you whether you want to think of yourself as the conservative share leader or the small competitor with mediocre share position and no leverage or, alternatively, as the agile market leader who reaps the rewards for approaching the market dramatically differently.

It doesn't require a wealth of financial, human, and physical resources to be a market leader and highly profitable disruptor:

- Uber, the world's largest taxi company (approximately $6.5 billion in annual revenues), owns no vehicles.

- Airbnb, the world's largest accommodations provider (approximately $2.8 billion in annual revenues), owns no real estate.

- Facebook, the world's most popular media owner (approximately $27.64 billion in annual revenues), provides no content.

- Alibaba, the world's most valuable retailer (approximately $5.6 billion in annual revenues), owns no inventory.

You can differentiate your brand by choosing to look at market leadership differently than your competitors. Developing your brand and disrupting the market around your unique .1% will enable you to improve your company's focus, alignment, engagement, and business results. Once you have identified your unique .1%, your next step is to craft your strategy to leverage it.

4

CRAFTING YOUR STRATEGY

We cannot manage what we cannot frame.
—Vaclav Smil

"If you don't know where you are going, any road will get you there," said the Cheshire Cat to Alice in Lewis Carroll's *Alice's Adventures in Wonderland*. And in the world of business, "any road" does not necessarily lead to success. In fact, failing to plan is planning to fail.

Strategic planning puts you in control of your organization's destiny. It enables you to make things happen *for* you, instead of merely allowing them happen *to* you.

Behind closed doors over the years, I've heard numerous mid-tier managers make statements like the following:

"Strategic planning is a waste of time. Senior leadership already has the numbers in mind they want us to hit to satisfy shareholders. We give them a PowerPoint that rationalizes what they want to see, so we can get our funding for next year and get back to work."

Obviously, these managers consider strategic planning to be a distraction from their "more urgent" day-to-day duties, rather than an exciting opportunity to chart a path for their company and themselves. Companies where this attitude prevails (which includes most) simply go through the motions for a few weeks each year. They come up with a plan, but they don't put much creativity or effort into crafting it, and therefore neither they nor their team members truly buy into it once it's completed.

Strategic planning puts you in control of your organization's destiny. It enables you to make things happen *for* you, instead of merely allowing them happen *to* you.

Let's pause here for a look in the mirror. If the senior leaders in your organization are handing down edicts on the plan, ask yourself why. How enthusiastically do *you* buy into the planning process? Do you find yourself giving less than your full commitment to it? Do you give them the impression that it is more of a nuisance than an opportunity? If so, you could be part of the problem. Your lack of commitment to planning might be sending a subtle message that you don't consider planning an important task. When you proactively take more ownership of the planning process by demonstrating more engagement, more excitement, and more innovative ideation, you will encourage senior leadership to give you more freedom in the development of the plan.

The most successful companies do an excellent job of crafting a strategic plan that becomes part of the fabric of the organization and serves as a guide for all of the organization's conversations, activities, and decisions. In my experience, these companies have highly engaged teams eager to follow their leaders. They are the types of companies that suppliers and new employees search out.

I have chosen the phrase "crafting a plan" because thoughtful planning requires the same degree of care that an artist might employ to carve a sculpture of wood. Both the wood craftsman and the strategic planner are creating something authentically personal. They both keep a vision in mind to guide their efforts, and they both cut away nonessential elements to arrive at the essence of that vision.

Your Strategic Plan

Too often top management makes the mistake of creating the plan and handing it down, expecting that others will enthusiastically execute it. It's no wonder that only 63% of companies on average deliver the financial performance they promised in their strategic plan.[4] Your strategic plan will have a greater probability of success if you allow the team who

> Your strategic plan will have a greater probability of success if you allow the team who will be executing it to have a hand in crafting it.

---

4   Michale C. Mankins and Richard Steele, "Turning Great Strategy into Great Performance," Harvard Business Review, July-August 2005

will be executing it to have a hand in crafting it. Participation in the creation of your plan instills a sense of ownership. Ownership stimulates initiative, innovation, and perseverance.

A properly conducted strategic planning process

- Aligns the organization with its foundational mission, vision, and values

- Looks beyond day-to-day urgencies to the long-term health of the business

- Creates organizational focus by providing a filter for priorities

- Creates a common communication platform to engage employees, suppliers, and customers

- Provides common benchmarks for establishing accountability and measuring success

Strategic Planning Is in Season

I've accepted the opportunity to coach quite a few different athletic teams. I find it very helpful to observe how college football coaches lead, guide, and mentor their players on and off the field. The way successful football coaches develop their game plan and emotionally lead their team is in many aspects analogous to the way successful business leaders develop a strategic plan and leverage it to engage and inspire their team to achieve the organization's goals.

Every coach has a vision for the season. Prior to the start of fall practices, a football coach and his staff will spend considerable time developing a comprehensive strategy that builds on that vision and the team's particular strengths. Once the overall game plan (strategy) is set, the coaches will assemble (recruit) the right players to execute the plan. At practice, they will have the players execute the plan again and again, because one player out of position on one play can cost the team a game, and one lost game can lead to negative momentum that spoils a season.

Prior to each game, the coaching staff will intensively study the opponent's strengths and weaknesses. Then they'll craft a specific plan for that game within the vision that best utilizes their team's strengths to attack that specific opponent's weaknesses. During the game, they will make adjustments as necessary from quarter to quarter, and even from series to series. Each game plan is somewhat flexible, but it always refers back to the overall strategy for the season, which in turn leverages the team's vision and particular strengths.

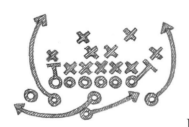 You can and should use this same type of diligent planning to craft a successful strategy for your business. Imagine how great it would be if your organization executed like a championship-caliber football team. How much more productively would your business function if all of your employees understood exactly what they were supposed to do and how their efforts contributed to the overall team? How much better would your employees perform if they were all fully committed to your company's strategy? How much would teamwork improve if all employees were aware of one another's goals and accountabilities? And how much more smoothly would operations flow if you huddled frequently as teams and in town hall meetings to refresh engagement, expectations, and assignments?

Obviously, executing your strategic plan as effectively as a championship football team would propel you ahead of your competition. Why then, in view of all these benefits, do so many managers consider strategic planning to be a tedious waste of time?

I believe that a portion of the blame for this apathy toward strategic planning should be directed at senior leaders. How can they expect managers to get excited about a top-down checklist process that requires very little creative thinking? It's the leader's responsibility to make the planning process relevant so team members will buy into it. Team members will only get excited about strategic planning if they understand how it will enable them to help accomplish the business's priorities and fulfill their own aspirations.

When I'm engaging with clients, I like to ask employees about their company's strategic plan. It's amazing (and disappointing) to see how few can explain its basic elements. Many can't even tell me the plan's critical priorities or what goals they are expected to achieve.

Homework Assignment

Conduct a survey of your team at your next team meeting.
Ask those in attendance to write their answers to the following questions:

(1) How would you describe the vision of our company?
(2) What are the three most important goals of our organization's annual plan?
(3) How does your position directly contribute to company goals?

Have everyone share their answers. (I guarantee that you will be surprised—and perhaps upset—by the lack of alignment.)

Defining Your Process

There is no singular approach to planning, and no one planning approach is best for every situation. There is a wrong approach to planning, however; it's to have no plan at all.

The strategic planning process is challenging enough, even when everyone is on the same page. But I've observed in my numerous business roles, both as an employee of organizations and as an outside consultant, that many of the problems with planning are due to confusion about the elements of the process. That's why I recommend starting every planning process with a team discussion of basic definitions. Many of my clients have found the following list and definitions of eight planning elements to be useful:

- **Mission:** The organization's fundamental purpose (usually phrased with respect to its customers, but ideally also with respect to its employees and the community)

- **Values:** Well-defined, deeply held beliefs about how the organization will behave (typically five to seven attributes, expressed in single words or short phrases)

- **Vision:** A verbal picture of what the organization desires to become, which will serve as a guide for both short- and long-term strategic planning (usually expressed as a simple, broad-based verbal narrative that projects out several years)

- **Goals:** Translations of the vision into short-term benchmarks useful for providing accountability and assessing progress (usually expressed as three to five overarching initiatives with high-level numbers that are aligned with the company's vision)

- **Objectives:** Two to three sub-goals for each goal that answer questions like how much and by when (expressed in very specific measurable quantities, such as units, time, share, and dollars)

- **Strategies:** The specific approaches the organization will use to attain its objectives (usually expressed as three to five overall initiatives)

- **Tactics:** The detailed activities the organization will execute to achieve its stated strategies (usually expressed as two to three activities per strategy)

- **Scorecard & Key Performance Indicators (KPIs):** Performance metrics (internal and external) for gauging the organization's overall health and its progress toward achieving its goals

Your choice of process will depend largely on the preferences and capabilities of your leadership team and the complexity of the environment in which your organization operates. But whatever method you use, make sure to ground your plan in your uniqueness, and design it to push you beyond your comfort zone. If your plan feels too comfortable, keep pushing your thinking. Evaluate the products, value chain, markets, customers, competitors, and other core components of your business with your "uniqueness filter" before including them in the plan. Factor into your plan the trends and gaps in your industry and the capabilities and tendencies of your competitors.

Be bold and courageous. Encourage your team to bring new and original ideas up for consideration or bring in disruptor consultants. Welcome any idea, as long as it's consistent with your organization's reason for existence. In every plan, force yourself to have some level of disruption, even if it means cannibalizing your own sales.

Setting the Foundation

First and foremost, know what you stand for. Why does your business exist? Your unique .1% will serve as the foundation for your strategy. It will specify for both you and your team where your business is going and how it will get there.

Mission, values, and vision are the foundational elements of your organization's strategy. As the word *foundation* implies, these elements will tend to be relatively stable over time. The most stable of these three elements is the mission, because it is the most fundamental embodiment of your company's reason to exist.

In the late 80s and 90s, mission statements were very much in vogue. It seems that every company had to have one. Management would gather a few senior people—often the wrong people— around a table and tell them to keep working until they had 100% agreement on a mission statement. Corporate leadership would then bless the document, get it printed up, and have HR post it on all the walls for employees, customers, and vendors to see. Once the company had checked this project off its to-do list, everyone would usually go back to business as usual.

Below is one such mission statement, which a company I'm familiar with now prominently posts in all of its offices:

> We pledge to serve every customer with the highest levels of sincerity, fairness, courtesy, respect and gratitude, delivered with unparalleled responsiveness, expertise, efficiency and accuracy. We are in business to create lasting relationships, and we will treat our customers like we want to be treated. We will offer the finest personal service and products delivered by caring team members who take 100% responsibility for meeting the needs of each customer.

Yawn! Have you ever read a more boring document? It checks off all the key points—sincerity, fairness, respect, etc., etc.—but it's not helpful because it could apply to just about any company. It is more of a laundry list of lofty ideals than a practical guide for decision making.

I'm in favor of mission statements when they are built on the organization's novel vision and clearly connect its goals to desired employee attitudes and behaviors. But unfortunately, most mission statements are so bland and generic they are basically useless. In fact, mission statements like the one on the previous page are freely available on the Internet. Some executives have confessed to me that their company got its mission statement, or at least the beginnings of it, just this way. Other companies have wasted money on "expert" HR marketing consultants who helped them develop a mission statement that could apply to just about any business.

I've gone into hundreds of companies and seen scores of mission statements. The great majority are displayed in dark corners, where they are simply gathering dust. Clearly, the organization's employees were not engaging or living with them. I've considered taking one of these mission statements off the wall of one company and swapping it with the mission statement from the wall of another company. I am quite certain that if I removed company names and logos, no one from either organization would notice the difference!

Why are the majority of mission statements so vacuous? I believe it's because they were developed by consensus. When you gather a group of people in a room and ask them to reach 100% agreement on a mission statement (or just about anything else, for that matter), you are setting the stage for bland mediocrity. In order to get unanimous agreement, everyone must feel comfortable with the content. But only the most watered-down mission statement will satisfy this criterion.

Mission statements should be original, challenging, and compelling. Their purpose is to provide focus and accountability, not comfort. A good mission statement stretches the thoughts and actions of the organization every day. A great one also makes people feel proud and a little uncomfortable, because it forces a different level of accountability and a different kind of thinking.

There are many types of mission statements, and no one way is right or wrong. But the best mission statements cover both the expectations of the external world and the internal team. Southwest Airlines, for example, does a great job of this:

> *The mission of Southwest Airlines is dedication to the highest quality of Customer Service delivered with a sense of warmth, friendliness, individual pride, and Company Spirit.*

The company follows its mission statement with a commitment to its employees:

> *We are committed to provide our Employees a stable work environment with equal opportunity for learning and personal growth. Creativity and innovation are encouraged for improving the effectiveness of Southwest Airlines. Above all, Employees will be provided the same concern, respect, and caring attitude within the organization that they are expected to share externally with every Southwest Customer.*

Casting Your Vision

As I mentioned at the beginning of this chapter, a company's vision is a verbal picture of what the organization desires to become. Your vision should leverage your company's unique .1% and serve as a guide for long-term strategic planning and operational plan investment. A worthwhile vision defines a future that inspires and energizes the organization.

Effective leaders cast visions that challenge the business to move forward imaginatively and boldly. They clearly and persuasively communicate the vision so employees will buy into it and understand their role in achieving it. Casting vision is an exciting process when properly executed. A vision that stretches the organization creates excitement for its employees because, in order to bring it to life, they will need to entertain new ideas and explore new frontiers.

One of your critical responsibilities as a leader is to weave your mission, vision, and values into the fabric of your organization as a solid and thoughtful foundation for your strategy. You must live these affirmations every day in every interaction. Simply posting them on your walls and reciting them in your literature and at random meetings produces little or no benefit. In fact, treating them as mere words can undermine the success of your strategy and even threaten the sustainability of your organization. Unfortunately, this is exactly what happened with Enron Corporation.

An Aborted Mission

Before its bankruptcy in December 2001, Houston-based Enron Corporation was one of the world's major utilities and communications companies, with about 20,000 employees and annual revenues in excess of $100 billion. For six consecutive years, *Fortune* had named it "America's Most Innovative Company." Enron proudly shared its stated mission, vision, and values with its employees, shareholders, and the public. They are spelled out below:

Mission

As a partner in the communities in which we operate, Enron believes it has a responsibility to conduct itself according to certain basic principles that transcend industries, cultures, economies, and local, regional and national boundaries. Because we take this responsibility as an international employer and global corporate citizen seriously, we have developed the following principles (values) on human rights: Respect, Integrity, Communications, and Excellence.

Vision

Enron's vision is to become the world's leading energy company—creating innovative and efficient energy solutions for growing economies and a better environment worldwide.

Values

Respect: We treat others as we would like to be treated ourselves. We do not tolerate abusive or disrespectful treatment. Ruthlessness, callousness and arrogance don't belong here.

Integrity: We work with customers and prospects openly, honestly and sincerely. When we say we will do something, we will do it; when we say we cannot or will not do something, then we won't do it.

Communication: We have an obligation to communicate. Here, we take the time to talk with one another...and to listen. We believe that information is meant to move and that information moves people.

Excellence: We are satisfied with nothing less than the very best in everything we do. We will continue to raise the bar for everyone. The great fun here will be for all of us to discover just how good we can really be.

Clearly, Enron didn't back up these words with the right actions and attitudes. Senior leadership focused on what they wanted the *public to see,* rather than on what they wanted the *company to be.* This "cracked foundation" undermined the organization's integrity and gave employees, customers, shareholders, and the public a false sense of security.

Ask yourself these questions:

- Does your company have a foundation of mission, vision, and values?

- If so, do all elements clearly communicate what you want to become?

- Do they capitalize on your unique .1%?

- Do they motivate you to make strategic decisions that will stretch you?

- Do they inspire you to reach for greater levels of achievement than you previously thought possible?

- Do they align with each other and with your overall reason to exist?

If you can't answer affirmatively to the above questions, your mission, values, and vision are probably not meaningful enough or aligned appropriately to your uniqueness. If your competitors would feel comfortable posting your mission statement on their website and office walls, your foundational elements are too generic. Go back to the beginning and make sure you have clearly identified your company's unique .1%. Then leverage this unique .1% into a solid foundation. Saturate the culture of your organization with these foundational elements, and hold people accountable (including suppliers) for living in accordance with them.

Once you have developed your foundational elements of mission, vision, and values, embody them in one original phrase that communicates the differentiated value your company offers to the market. This is your company's value proposition, or brand promise. Communicate it clearly and live it daily.

An On-Target Proposition

In the branding class I teach at the University of Notre Dame's Mendoza School of Business, I always ask students at the beginning of each quarter whether they shop at Target. Founded in Minneapolis, Minnesota, in 1902, the Target Corporation is the third largest discount retailer in the world, with more than 1,800 stores and annual revenues close to $70 billion. So, it's not surprising that invariably many hands go up. When I next ask the students how closely their purchases match their shopping list, most will say that they go into the store with a list of one or two items, but they end up doing a lot of browsing and come out with several purchases.

"There's nothing unusual about that," you might be saying to yourself. "We all tend to spend more time and money in stores than we intend." That's true, but Target is an exceptional case, boasting much higher than average shopping cart conversion rates. And the reason is not an accident. It's due to the company's very intentional execution of its strategy.

Target's unique .1% is to be a retailer of original styles not found on any other cost-effective retail platform. The company sums up its customer philosophy in the following value proposition:

> Expect More. Pay Less.
> *More great designs, more choices, and more designer items*
> *you won't find anywhere else. And pay less.*
> *It's as simple as that.*

Target requires its vendors to supply it with new, trend-setting styles at least annually and always on an exclusive basis. Consequently, its stores are regularly phasing in stylish new products in numerous categories and displaying them in engaging ways. My students say they sometimes walk around a Target store for hours, looking at all the new designs and getting excited and inspired by all of the colors and fashions they don't find anywhere else. The store's original designs are not limited to apparel products; they're found in all categories, such as lighting, housewares, gardening, and even pet supplies. That's why a shopper who comes in for bed sheets and a CD may end up buying several other cool, newly designed items in housewares or furniture.

This strategy has made Target a market leader. The company has advanced the retail experience by bringing boutique design and aesthetic expectation into mass merchandising. Ikea has used this "affordable luxury" approach to become one of the largest furniture retailers.

The Price of Success

Walmart, the world's largest retailer with annual revenues of almost $485 billion and more than two million employees, has found success on the other end of the spectrum. Its vision is to offer the largest selection of products at the most cost-effective prices. It embodies this unique .1% in the value proposition, "We save people money so they can live better."

In contrast to Target, which requires its suppliers to provide exclusive designs, Walmart's purchasing contracts stipulate that vendors must furnish a predetermined incremental percentage (usually 1% to 3%) of sustainability savings every year. Walmart can deliver on its brand promise to shoppers, because its vendors are under continual pressure to manufacture, package, and deliver products more sustainably and economically.

Target and Walmart have extremely successful strategies. They both have built their brand promise around their unique .1%, and their employees and suppliers deliver on that brand promise. As a result, their customers know exactly what to expect. That's why their shoppers typically spend substantial amounts of money on each shopping trip.

Stuck in the Middle

Kmart has been less successful than both Target or Walmart because it tried to walk a middle road between them. The worst strategic position is in the middle. The most successful businesses stand out from their competitors; they own a distinct and exclusive space based on their unique .1%.

> The worst strategic position is in the middle. The most successful businesses stand out from their competitors; they own an exclusive space based on their unique .1%.

On one hand, Kmart attempted to imitate Walmart's low-price strategy by offering "Blue Light Specials." As customers were shopping, blue lights would occasionally flash in the store to indicate special sales. This was supposed to excite bargain hunters, but it mostly confused them. When the blue lights began flashing, it was difficult to know which products were going on sale. This strategy was also less effective than couponing, which allows customers to pre-plan purchases. Kmart discontinued "Blue Light Specials" a few years ago, but recently I was surprised to read that the company is bringing them back. Kmart may consider this idea unique, but *unique only works if it's relevant.*

On the other hand, Kmart attempted to imitate Target by stocking celebrity apparel and home furnishings. But this aspect of their strategy also failed, because its stores carried only a couple of categories of designer products, and people weren't inclined to walk through the rest of the store. Besides, even these designs were usually months behind the fashion trends.

Recently, Kmart announced that it has begun amassing goods from bankrupt companies and other "opportunistic situations" and reselling them at discounted prices. The company calls this entry into the liquidation business "innovative and brag-worthy," but I think it's a desperate strategy that will push the struggling retailer deeper into the abyss of marketplace irrelevance.

Kmart's strategy is failing because the company is trying to play in the middle and imitate the strategies of its competitors, instead of identifying and leveraging its own unique .1%. Rather than taking a solid stand, its approach confuses customers. The results are starkly apparent: discouraging sales results, uncommitted customers, unengaged employees, and dissatisfied shareholders.

Long-term success doesn't simply happen by reducing prices, improving quality, or marginally improving on what already exists in some other way. It results from embodying your .1% in a value proposition, and then following through on that value proposition with your customers, vendors, and employees. The most successful companies develop a vision and strategy around their reason to exist that is relevant to their target audience. Then they continually seek to optimize that strategy as they execute it in the face of evolving conditions in the marketplace. Companies who fail to identify their own uniqueness end up constantly chasing their competitors and consistently struggling to build a sustainable brand or business.

> The most successful companies develop a vision and strategy around their reason to exist that is relevant to their target audience.

Successful companies continually evolve with the changing demands of the marketplace. For example, both Target and Walmart are almost certainly assessing their strategies, as Amazon and other online retailers zero in on their customer base and product categories.

Best Buy has also been experiencing declining profitability in recent years due to online competition. To stay relevant in today's marketplace, which demands ever-increasing levels of service, so as to avoid ending up like Circuit City and CompUSA, it has doubled down on its unique .1% of providing technical support for customers. For example, the company's Geek Squad currently makes about 4 million house calls per year to help customers install and manage their entertainment systems. By reemphasizing technical support, which online retailers do not provide, and by implementing various other management and strategy enhancements, Best Buy seems to be regaining its former profitability.

Strategic Planning Missteps

I'm concluding this chapter by talking about four strategic

planning mistakes that many companies commit, possibly because they don't know better, or because they aren't thorough enough in their planning process.

The first strategic planning mistake is prioritizing showmanship over leadership. During the planning process, some managers go all out to make their presentations sparkle. They know that the most lavish presentations usually get the most attention and praise. Not infrequently, they unfortunately also get the quickest approvals.

Your organization can avoid this error by looking both backward and forward in the planning process. When assessing your future plans, hold people accountable for their past performance. Require leaders to clearly verbalize your business's reason to exist. Deemphasize showmanship and focus on novel insights, vision, and business acumen. Reward bold thinking and business results, not smooth talk and flashy PowerPoint presentations that many leaders hide behind. Make your employees have a true business conversation.

The second strategic planning error is failure to start afresh each year. Instead of using zero-based planning, many companies simply rework the previous year's plan. They allow managers to present plans year after year that are essentially identical, except for updated numbers. This "cloning" method of planning can cause the company to overlook changing market dynamics, trends, and new opportunities.

Even if you've followed essentially the same plan for the past three years (or even the past 20 years!), don't assume it's the best plan for next year. In any 12-month period, much can change about your company, your customers, your market, your industry, and the overall economy. Always employ zero-based strategic planning to ensure that you consider all substantive changes that have occurred since you developed your last plan. Take into account all important new market gaps and trends that are likely to impact your approach in the future. And very importantly, remember to filter all this optimization planning through your organization's foundational elements.

The third strategic planning mistake is failure to develop contingency plans for unforeseen changes, both bad and good. One of my managers used to call this contingency planning the "Oh, crap!" process. When you hear this expression, you know something has gone wrong that you didn't expect.

I recommend developing contingency plans for both negative and positive "oh, crap" scenarios. On the negative side, plan what you would do if you lost, say, 20% to 35% of your revenues? What actions would you take in your channels, geographic markets, product mix, and organization to regain the right amount of business? How would you adjust your business if this decrease was going to be the new norm?

Then plan for the contingency of growing your business 20% to 35% over forecast. Most companies don't do this, and it's very important to think through in advance what additional people and resources you would need and how you would get them. Having these contingency plans in place for both positive and negative scenarios will give you confidence and allow you to react quickly to emerging trends and unexpected events. Contingency planning empowers you to be proactive instead of merely reactive. A contingency plan costs money to develop and quickly execute, but before you allow this to deter you, I challenge you to consider the risks and potential costs of not having one.

The fourth and most egregious mistake in strategic planning is failure to conduct scenario planning. As you and the rest of your planning team sit around your conference table crafting your plan, be aware that your competitors are doing something very similar. Since companies in the same industry are typically 99.9% identical, it's very likely that they are creating similar new products and exploring similar growth opportunities, while plotting how to take share from you in key markets and accounts. Don't assume they are going to sit still and simply allow you to execute your strategy. Every major action you take will spark a reaction.

Prepare a comprehensive scenario plan at least annually that considers how the competition will likely react to your annual plans and proposed actions, and attach these to your strategic plan assumptions. Competitive scenario planning is one of the most helpful, but also one of the most underutilized, business planning practices. When conducted appropriately and over time, scenario planning will uncover a great deal internally and externally and put you in a much stronger position to succeed.

For example, if you plan to grow by 5% in some segment of your market, your team should do comprehensive scenario planning about how your competitors might react. What market segments will they try hardest to protect? Which ones are they likely to care less about? When we think through competitive scenarios as part of the strategic planning process with our clients, we turn a conference room into a war room and fill the walls with decision tree diagrams. Taking a page from Sun Tzu's *The Art of War*, we use this process to make us more knowledgeable and effective in battling our competition and serving our customers.

Crafting a strategic plan is hard work, but it is critical for success. Assign your best strategic thinkers to the task. Craft a strategy that leverages your uniqueness and builds on a deep understanding of your industry, your competition (current and potential future), and relevant trends. A diligently developed plan serves as a valuable focus and filter for effective actions and a platform for sustainable growth. Rally your whole team around your common focus by sharing your vision with them early and often, especially whenever you enhance your vision to fit changing market dynamics.

Creating a comprehensive plan is just a start; it doesn't guarantee success. In subsequent chapters, you will learn how to think differently about taking your strategy to a new level. We will discuss how to engage your team and how to engage the market, so you can achieve and even exceed your planned goals and dramatically outperform your market.

5

DRIVING SUSTAINABLE GROWTH

This is your world; shape it, or someone else will.
—Gary Lew

Growth is the lifeblood of every business. Without growth, a company will have limited ability to invest in new products, implement new processes, acquire new technologies, hire new employees, and pursue other promising opportunities. Growth leads to larger revenues that help spread fixed costs over more units of production, increasing both profit margins and net profits. But don't just pursue growth for the sake of growth. Pursue only

the growth that is purposeful and closely aligned with the overall vision and strategy of your business.

Your growth strategy should have both offensive and defensive components. The *offensive* component should be intentional and 100% aligned with your strategy. It should fill in the holes in the channels and categories where you see opportunity to leverage your uniqueness. Identify a very specific and measurable growth goal, so your entire organization can have a laser focus on achieving it. Encourage your team to look at your business and your industry with fresh eyes. Their alertness to trends, gaps, and opportunities in the market will help them take ownership of the growth strategy and keep your products relevant. This will ultimately result in higher revenues and profits for your business.

The average business loses around 20% of its customers annually simply by failing to attend to customer relationships.[5] Ideally, your churn will be lower than that, but inevitably your business will experience some customer defections. The defensive component of your growth strategy should spell out in considerable detail the structure and approach by market, customer type, channel, and product mix that you plan to take to offset these involuntary revenue losses.

Your plan should also spell out your policy for voluntarily shedding undesirable customers, such as those who don't meet your profitability standards or those who don't fit with your vision or business model. Develop plans for replacing lost business with business that's better aligned with your strategy. However, don't

---

5   20 Customer Retention Strategies [Web log post]. Retrieved from
     http://marketingwizdom.com/strategies/retention-strategies

devote so much attention to protecting your current customer base that you neglect your offensive strategy.

As we said in the last chapter, faster-than-forecast growth is a better problem than too little growth, but it's still a problem. "Oh, crap, I can't fill all the orders!" is not something you want to hear your team saying. Have a detailed contingency plan for how you will rapidly scale up capacity and resources. The cost of keeping this contingency plan in place will be modest compared to the tangible and intangible costs of failing to fill incremental orders in markets where you want to grow.

If you are unable to expand your production capacity to fulfill an increasing volume of orders, evaluate the products you currently manufacture. Be willing to shed less profitable SKUs to free up capacity for

> Pursue only the growth that is purposeful and closely aligned with the overall vision and strategy of your business.

more profitable and trending (early life cycle) ones. If you don't want to discontinue a product, consider having another company produce it under your label. In recent years, more and more businesses in almost every industry are successfully subcontracting some production to their competitors. This strategy may sound risky, but it's actually a great way to use your in-house capacity to grow your most profitable products, without taking your less-profitable ones off the market.

Profiting From the Right Growth

Growth is about more than just increasing revenues. It should be about enhancing your profits and the profits of your customers. I understand that growing a commodity product may help you spread your fixed costs, but it also can divert your focus and resources away from higher-end sales opportunities. Most companies primarily focus their sales efforts on their commodity (or "good") products. They call these SKUs the bread and butter of their offering. However, I prefer optimizing the overall mix. Go beyond increasing revenues and start optimizing profitability. The goal of any business should be to optimize profit share, not merely market share (volume/unit).

Homework Assignment

Have your team do an assessment of your market share by channel, audience type, product mix, and geographic area. (If the data you need is not readily available, you have another homework assignment!) Calculate the profitability of each to gauge where you are positioned with respect to blended industry profit share.

Optimizing profit is like a chess match, but you must have a thorough knowledge of your industry and your competitors to play the game. For example, one of the best ways to dramatically increase your profits is to optimize your product and/or channel mix. I call this the "hidden gem" of growth, because not many business leaders stop to calculate the large potential impact of a slight shift in mix. Optimizing channel mix is more difficult than optimizing product mix because channels are subject to more influences and afford you less control. The following discussion will primarily focus on product mix.

> The goal of any business should be to optimize profit share, not merely market share (volume/unit).

I have found through my experience with hundreds of manufacturers that the product offerings of most companies can be classified as shown on the chart below. Typically, they derive about 75% of their revenues and 40% of their profits from commodity products. The "better" mid-tier products furnish about 20% of sales and approximately 30% of profits. But the real heroes are the top-tier ("best") products, which typically have the most value to end users and are at the front end of their product life cycle. Even though they represent only about 5% of total units sold, they can contribute an amazing 30% or so to the company's total profits.

As the right column in the illustration below demonstrates, growing your sales in the best category by a mere 1% will drive profits up 6%. In contrast, revenues of good products would have to increase 12% to achieve this same level of incremental profitability. Obviously, it would require considerably more marketing, manufacturing, and other resources to sell 12% more good products than it would to sell 1% more best products. The conclusion is clear: To most easily increase your overall profitability, leverage your high-value products.

	% Unit Sales	% Total Profit	Profit % Impact from 1% Unit Sales Increase
BEST	5%	30%	6%
BETTER	20%	30%	1.5%
GOOD	75%	40%	.5%

Homework Assignment

If you haven't already analyzed your products as described earlier, I urge you to do so. You may be surprised to see the positive impact you can make on your profitability with only a modest change of organizational focus and investment of resources.

Growth Strategies

Some managers are content to let their business simply drift along with the market, because it's usually far simpler to maintain growth than to intentionally build it. If the overall market goes up 5% and doesn't experience any major shifts, these managers count on their business growing by approximately 5% as well.

This strategy—if it can be considered a strategy—is called **average market growth**, or **organic growth**. It requires limited skill, creativity, and investment. Ultimately, the company is at the whim of its industry's natural momentum, with limited control over its own destiny. Shareholders expect to benefit from positive average market growth, but they look to invest in companies that continually demonstrate they can outperform the market and achieve a higher pace of growth than merely what the market will give them.

A second growth strategy, and probably the most common, is referred to as **market share gain**. In this scenario, the company's goal is to take market share ("buy" market share might be a more accurate description) from its competitors. Since most companies in the same industry have similar products and services, the competitive battle invariably falls back to the lowest common denominator: price. When one company cuts prices, other companies usually retaliate. Back and forth it goes, creating a "domino effect" that ultimately leads to lower revenues and profits for all suppliers. The only winners in the share-game approach are the customers who receive the lower prices for a period of time.

A third growth strategy employs **acquisitions and joint ventures** (AJV). This is typically the most complex and expensive approach. Merging the different people, policies, procedures, visions, and cultures of two companies is always challenging, and sometimes painful. This is especially true when the acquiring company lacks a strongly established culture and vision. AJV is also the riskiest approach with a failure rate of somewhere between 70% and 90%.[6] But if it gets you more quickly into a new category that can leverage your .1%, then it can make sense.

I have been involved in several acquisitions, and the business benefits rarely match initial expectations. Even when two companies have compatible cultures and visions, which is extremely rare, the purchaser must invariably make many adjustments concerning personnel, manufacturing assets, marketing, and culture. Most of these adjustments have a dampening effect on engagement and profitability. That's why it's so important *prior* to an acquisition to build a foundation for success on a deep company culture, a well-defined vision, and a strong strategic planning process.

Creating Demand

As you can tell, I'm not overly enthusiastic about the three most common methods of growth outlined above. I will accept *average market growth*, because it requires limited incremental effort and resources. At times I might play the *market share gain* game, but only if I can swap some of my existing commodity share for share

---

6   "The Big Idea: The New M&A Playbook," by Clayton M. Christensen, Richard Alton, Curtis Rising, and Andrew Waldeck, March 2011, Harvard Business Review. Retrieved at https://hbr.org/2011/03/the-big-idea-the-new-ma-playbook

that is more profitable. I am always happy to give my competition low-margin share, while I take the more profitable share. But when I use this approach, I will thoroughly think through the scenarios of my own strategy and how competitors might react to my company's actions.

Finally, I will occasionally consider an *acquisition or joint venture,* but only if I am convinced after much scrutiny that the deal will be sustainably profitable, consistent with my company's vision, and aligned with favorable trends. I'll also be more favorably inclined toward an AJV if it offers an entry into a market where trends tell me I should increase my placement.

The Power of Demand Creation

While not overly enamored with these three growth strategies, I am passionate about a more impactful growth strategy that only a few select companies utilize. Companies who are better at maintaining momentum than building it will find this approach challenging to execute. In fact, they may find it difficult to comprehend why any company would want to pursue it. This strategy is called **demand creation**, and it's one of the best kept secrets in business.

The sole focus of demand creation is to create demand for your *industry.* It's about making the overall industry pie bigger, instead of merely shifting more share to your company within a fixed market size. This strategy is unappealing to many business leaders because it seems counterintuitive. "Why should we invest our money in making the whole pie bigger?" they say. "If the whole market gets bigger, that will also help our competitors. Why would we invest resources to help our competitors grow?"

These skeptics fail to realize two key points. First, the new demand you create typically generates higher than normal profits because most products at the beginning of their life cycle sell better and can command higher prices. Second, the company responsible for enlarging the pie invariably ends up with a disproportionately larger slice of the bigger pie.

Your goal in creating more demand in your industry is to advance the category and ultimately capture a very large share of that newly created demand for yourself. But you must first focus on using the gaps and insights you have identified to create a relevant approach that will enlarge the overall demand in the industry. If you bypass industry growth and attempt to create demand for yourself, you'll simply be reverting to the second or third growth strategy previously mentioned and not leverage the entirety of the momentum an industry can create.

Disrupting the Norm

As I have said, one major reason why very few companies use the demand creation growth strategy is because the concept seems counterintuitive. A second and perhaps even bigger reason is because demand creation is disruptive. It challenges conventional wisdom and the customary processes of your company and your industry, and it may drastically alter some of the B2B relationships you have cultivated over numerous years. Most people are conflict averse; they prefer comfort to disruption.

In order to successfully create demand, a company needs to cultivate a culture that encourages disruptive thinking. Its leaders must learn to be comfortable with being uncomfortable. They need to go beyond merely tolerating change to actually embracing it. They must continually be on the lookout for novel, even radical new opportunities for achieving growth, and they must be willing to pursue the most promising opportunities, even when they lead in unsettling directions.

Demand creation requires exceptional commitment and tenacity. Companies that excel at it look for employees who tend to think differently and embrace disruption, and they commission them to be "champions" of long-term, significant change. Successful demand creation champions are extraordinarily insightful, creative thinkers who can see possibilities that others overlook. They have the confidence to speak up, even when it means challenging years of company tradition and pushing back against senior leadership. Companies committed to demand creation will strive to have at least one of these champions in every important company meeting as a catalyst.

> Its leaders must learn to be comfortable with being uncomfortable.

The most enjoyable (and challenging) position I ever held was Director of Demand Creation at Owens Corning. The CEO wholeheartedly believed in the value of disruption, and he gave my team the mandate and the freedom to devote 100% of our time to thinking differently and developing new insights about our business and our industry. As a result, we were able to discern important trends and gaps that helped us uncover several innovative opportunities.

Unfortunately, many companies put so much emphasis on maintaining low headcount that they are reluctant to commission a fulltime demand-creation individual, let alone a demand-creation team. If your business cannot dedicate resources to this endeavor, at least consider designating a few imaginative thinkers to be demand-creation champions. Give them the freedom and responsibility to challenge the status quo as they continue to carry out their regular job responsibilities.

I urge you, however, to regard this fallback position as merely an admirable start. When you commission people to spend 10% to 20% of their time on anything, they will eventually go back to spending 100% of their time on their main responsibility. Shared resource approaches are usually ineffective. You'll get much better results and send a stronger message to the organization when you make a full commitment to the concept of demand creation by dedicating resources to it. I guarantee that the positive cultural change and enhanced business benefits this investment can produce will far outweigh the incremental headcount costs.

Sometimes the demand creation champions you need will already be on your company's payroll. You simply must uncover them, enable them to spread their wings by releasing them from the handcuffs of the organization, and let them soar. But I often find that existing employees have difficulty breaking away from familiar and comfortable ways of thinking. For this reason, you may want to hire experienced change agents who have fewer preconceived notions about your company and industry. Look for people who are able and willing to stretch your company's thinking beyond the usual approaches. Investing in just a few demand creation champions—two to three might initially be sufficient for a company of 10,000 employees—can have a huge impact on the future growth and sustainable success of your business.

A Culture of Possibility

In my role as Director of Demand Creation, my main goal was to create millions of dollars of *incremental* new business in the industry. To drive a culture of possibility, I would start every meeting by saying, "What would you do if you knew you wouldn't fail?" My objective was to get the team into the right frame of mind by clearing away all the pre-existing corporate baggage and handcuffs.

Once we found a new path to create incremental demand, our team worked with the established division leaders to help define an approach to capture a disproportionately large share of this new business. It was exciting work, but definitely not easy. I sometimes felt like I spent the majority of my time explaining what the heck demand creation was and why our actions made sense. Many internally considered the whole idea more of a nuisance than an exciting opportunity. I seemed to be constantly justifying my team's existence.

Most employees in the company (including some in leadership) had difficulty grasping the concept of demand creation, especially rule #1, which is to focus first on the industry and not on the company. This resistance is not unusual. When you challenge management's traditional ways of doing things, the typical response is something like, "Don't disturb our natural rhythm. We've already got our path. Besides, why should we spend time on something new that puts our existing business at risk?"

I've found it's usually easier to sell revolutionary new ideas like demand creation externally than internally. Employees are prone to say things like, "We can't do that in our business," or "That's not the way things have been done in this industry." Such negative reactions indicate that leadership is not giving enough priority to continually stretching the organization's vision of why it exists.

Shortly after I assumed my position, we brought in Gap International, a consulting firm that specializes in organizational transformation. Over several months, Gap's team conducted numerous meetings to teach our company's leaders how to think differently about leadership and opportunity. During a meeting break, I shared with the presenter the difficulties I was having getting my own organization to think differently about market opportunity. The conversation gave me a simple but revelatory insight that has impacted the way I look at business growth. I share it with you below, because it can help you grow your company at a rate you might have previously considered impossible:

> *If you have a $10 million business, and you want to grow to $100 million in three to five years, you have to start thinking and acting like a $100 million business TODAY. You can't get there by merely talking about it. It won't work to simply announce your goals with impressive PowerPoint presentations and elaborate Excel spreadsheets, while conducting business as usual. Merely tweaking what you've always done may get you to $12 million or $15 million, but it won't get you to $100 million. Be bold, adventurous, and willing to live outside your comfort zone.*

Over the years, I have come to deeply believe that growing a successful business is fundamentally about creating and embedding a "culture of possibility" throughout the entire organization. To reach your goal of $100 million, the company needs to start identifying bigger gaps, making bigger decisions, hiring different thinkers, taking greater risks, and

...growing a successful business is fundamentally about creating and embedding a "culture of possibility" throughout the entire organization.

seeking bigger opportunities, so its actions align with and augment its bigger goal. Senior leadership and the company's team members must all cultivate this culture of possibility, so it flourishes in every meeting and in every conversation.

Our demand-creation team put posters on the walls of our meeting rooms to remind us that words like *but, devil's advocate, never,* and *can't* had been banned from our vocabulary. Such "self-limiting" words stifle differentiated thinking and destroy a culture of possibility.

Constructing New Growth

I greatly admire industry leaders who have the foresight and courage to get out of their comfort zones and invest their resources in groundbreaking initiatives, and I was privileged to work in this environment at Owens Corning. Perhaps the best way for me to explain demand creation is to tell you about a project team I was asked to lead.

Owens Corning is a leading manufacturer of insulation materials for the building industry and our team's mission was to create greater demand for insulation materials in existing homes. We focused on existing homes rather than newly constructed homes because they represented a greater market opportunity at a reasonable project cost to the homeowner.

The easiest and most economical way to increase the insulation in an existing home is by adding insulation to the attic. Most homes have some insulation in the attic, but the level in older homes is usually insufficient to meet modern building codes for energy efficiency and comfort.

At that time, the reality was that only about two million U.S. homeowners re-insulated their attics each year, and Owens Corning already had a dominant share of this market. Even if we captured a 5% greater share from our competitors, we would re-insulate only 100,000 more attics per year. This goal wouldn't help us grow exponentially, and we'd probably have to cut prices and profits to achieve it. Competitors would retaliate by cutting their prices, which would negatively impact overall category profits. The only winners would be the customers receiving the discounts. Clearly, this "buying market share" approach was an unacceptable growth option.

So, we decided to think differently. To start, we decided that the strongest candidates for re-insulation were houses 20 or more years old. Through our research, we learned that approximately 65% of the 110 million homes in

> *Possibility market* is the share of the market that we could ultimately possibly capture, not merely the share of the market that is currently being captured.

the U.S. fell into this age category. We began to consider our potential market for re-insulating attics to be approximately 70 million homes per year (65% x 110 million). We called this our *"possibility market." Possibility market* is the share of the market that we could ultimately possibly capture, not merely the share of the market that is currently being captured. A possibility market of 70 million homes was quite an increase from a traditionally defined (addressable) market of two million homes!

Our new perspective dramatically changed the way we viewed our market and our share within it. We had previously thought of ourselves as owning a large portion of a market of two million attics per year, but by thinking of the possibility market as 70 million homes, we realized our "possibility share" was less than 1% of the holistic market. Just by thinking differently about possibility, we immediately saw a much more exciting opportunity and challenge. The question now became, what can we do to increase the number of homeowners who re-insulate their attics each year? In other words, how can we create more demand in the overall market?

Forward March!

My first step was to set a HUG (Huge Unthinkable Goal) that would in normal planning be considered extraordinarily optimistic. Our HUG was to increase the number of attics the industry would re-insulate from two million to three million per year. If we had considered our market to be the two million attics that are customarily re-insulated each year, an additional one million attics would have represented a 50% increase. No one would have bought into that impossible goal!

But from a possibility share perspective, we only had to increase our share of the 70-million-home market by 1.4% (one million / 70 million opportunity). That sounded a lot more doable. So, I organized a campaign that I coined the "1 Million Attic March." Our goal was to motivate my team, my company, our customers, and the industry to insulate just one million incremental attics per year. (Yes, I intentionally used the word "just"!)

Up to this point, our team had simply enlarged its view of the market and developed measurable marching orders. While that was huge, it was the simple part. Now we had to find the right approach for actually creating this new demand. To start off, we needed to understand why only two million homeowners were adding insulation to their attics, when actually 70 million homes needed it. Was it due to lack of interest, lack of awareness, lack of urgency, or lack of finances? Our research revealed it was a combination of all of these.

Based on this information, we looked for ways to convince homeowners that attic re-insulation was easy and important. We decided that the simplest approach would be to create a turnkey process that would enable professionals to diagnose the insulation levels of homeowners' attics while they were already in their homes. They would then be able to give homeowners an estimate of their energy-bill savings from re-insulation, inform them about the greater comfort they could expect, quote a price on the spot, and do a quick install using a process that would cause limited disruption in the home.

With this in mind, we approached the insulation contractors we had as customers. They already had the equipment, the knowhow, and the laborers to do insulation jobs. But we experienced a huge "ah-ha" when we learned that these contractors on average spent 95% of their time working on new construction installations. They would typically descend on the construction site with their big trucks and crews of installers, dressed in well-worn overalls and heavy boots. It didn't matter that these installers bumped into walls and engaged in "colorful" conversations while dragging equipment from room to room, because the walls were unfinished, there were no homeowners on the scene to hear the conversations, and there were no pieces of furniture to damage.

We attempted to convince these contractor companies to enter the repair and remodel (R&R) market to take advantage of this new demand we were creating, and we even offered them training and support. But it soon became obvious that this market would present an enormous challenge for most of them. For one thing, they had no experience in marketing or selling to homeowners. They didn't know how to create leads or how to appropriately provide services when owners were present in their nicely furnished, crowded homes.

Furthermore, these contractors had not trained their installers to interface with homeowners. Their crews didn't understand the importance of appearance, and most of them would have balked at wearing uniforms and the protective shoe coverings needed to prevent staining of carpets and scratching of floors. Still another problem was that although the large trucks and insulation rigs used by these contractors worked fine with houses under construction with no cars in driveways, they were not suitable for servicing busy, populated neighborhoods.

Some of the contractors we talked to did successfully start a new business model around R&R, but they had to develop a new strategy and hire new people to do it. The vast majority were not able, or were simply not willing, to make the transition.

Success in the Home

We took a step back and asked ourselves, "So, if we can't count on these contractors, who else understands how to market, sell, and install products into existing homes?" It then dawned on us that we needed to go to the contractors who had specialized in R&R for years. They were in homes every day selling and installing products such as windows, roofing, siding, HVAC. They knew how to generate leads and sell the value of their products while sitting across the kitchen table from homeowners. We simply had to make it easy for these R&R contractors to take on this new business model of installing insulation in attics. To make this happen, we put the wheels in motion to give them insulation products, training, and marketing materials.

However, we soon encountered a major hurdle. These R&R contractors needed installation equipment compact enough to fit in their existing trucks and vans. So, we partnered with a design firm and developed a new piece of equipment to install insulation in attics. We called it the *AttiCat*™, and along with it, we developed a new type of insulation that worked only with this machine. Taking a page from the razor and razor blades marketing playbook, the *AttiCat* machine was our razor, and the packages of insulation material were our blades.

Our next step was to introduce the *AttiCat* concept to the R&R contractors and show them how they could use it to augment their existing services to homeowners. They immediately saw the advantage of picking up an extra $1,500 to $2,000 for a re-insulation project while they were already installing an $8,000 roof, a $12,000 siding project, or a $20,000 window package.

Our "1 Million Attic March" campaign came to fruition at the perfect time: right before the abrupt decline in the new-construction housing market. Contractors were looking for new business lines to add to their offering, and we gave them the products they needed and the support to use them. Because the *AttiCat* machine paid for itself after a modest number of projects, hundreds of new contractors entered the attic insulation-installation business.

Our initiative was so successful that it was only a matter of time before our competitors followed with their own machines and products. But as the leader in developing this concept, we captured a disproportionately large share of the incremental demand we had created in the industry. What's more, our innovative approach advanced the whole category and clearly enhanced our reputation as the industry leader, which in turn boosted the sales of our other product categories. This is just one example of the power of demand creation and the advantage of looking at your market from the perspective of possibility share rather than market share.

Your Possibility Share

With our *AttiCat* approach, we stretched the industry's view of what is possible. The industry was accustomed to using "total current installations/year" figures like those below to gauge the annual size of the U.S. market for R&R services per category:

Product Category	Total Current Installations/Year	% of Possibility Market
Entry Doors	7.5 million units	10%
Roofing	4.5 million roofs	6%
Garage Doors	2.0 million projects	3%
Decking	2.0 million projects	3%
Attic Re-insulation	2.0 million attics	3%

When our clients learned to view the potential market as the 70 million homes that were more than 20 years old, they realized that, for example, the 7.5 million entry doors installed each year represented only 10% of the possible market. Not all manufacturers in this industry shifted their focus from the historical definition of market share to the new concept of possibility share. But when some adopted this new view and realized that 90% or more of their market was untapped latent demand, they began to play the role of market leader, ultimately advancing the category and their own business results.

We promoted the concept of possibility share throughout the entire value chain—from the national manufacturers of products down to the local contractors. For example, when I was the featured speaker at a trade show, I challenged the 350 contractors in my audience to utilize this concept in their local markets. I asked them, "What would your business look like and how would you approach your market differently if your opportunity grew by 25%, 50%, or even 100%?" Some of these contractors accepted my challenge and began viewing their market differently. Some who remained in contact told me they found new ways to exploit untapped potential in their geographic regions and product categories. They reported dramatic increases in sales and, more importantly, in profits.

Changing your definition of what is possible can dramatically stretch your team's vision. As the leader, your next challenge is to get your team to pursue this new vision with energy, creativity, and perseverance. Once they take ownership of the concept, you will almost certainly experience dramatic improvement in engagement levels and business results.

6

LEADING FROM VISION

The task of the leader is to get his people from
where they are to where they have not been.
–Henry A. Kissinger

Practically every leadership book defines leadership differently.
But at a fundamental level, they all essentially agree that
leadership is about action. I define leadership as the act of moving
something forward. Of advancing an entity or cause to a higher
level of performance. Business professionals, government officials,
military commanders, teachers, athletic and executive coaches,
mentors, and other leaders all enjoy the privilege of leading
individuals and organizations forward to a better place.

The role of an organizational leader is to stretch the team and its
members to a place beyond what they previously thought possible.

Outstanding leaders do this by helping their followers understand the organization's overall purpose (mission), its destination (vision), how people should behave as they move forward (values), the key milestones along the way (goals), and the actions required to achieve the goals (strategies). They develop all of these around the organization's unique .1%, and they make sure the overall mission and vision of the organization aligns with that of the organizational unit they are leading. Finally, they establish accountability to

> ...leadership as the act of moving something forward, of advancing an entity or cause to a higher level of performance.

ensure that everyone works effectively on initiatives critical to the vision, and they do their best to clear away obstacles that hinder progress. Employees engaged in this manner will own the success of the plan. With this level of commitment, there will be very few limits on what they can accomplish.

I have been granted the opportunity to lead thousands of people in my business career. Each of these leadership roles has been very rewarding. They have taught me a great deal and provided a solid foundation for my leadership maturation process. I have also been blessed to parent four biological children along with more than 20 foster children. What a joy and privilege it has been to love, nurture, guide, mentor, and provide for them! How fulfilling it has been to help them grow into adults of good character who make wise choices. (Well, usually!) When they come home for the holidays, I still say to them as they walk out the door to visit friends, "Make good decisions." Once a parent, always a parent!

Good parents cast a vision for their children, and then they exemplify the core principles necessary to attain that vision. By their faithful presence, they help their children through the various challenges they will inevitably encounter. By providing sound counsel at appropriate times, they help them develop into amazing adults whose lives will positively impact others.

Exceptional organizational leaders function somewhat like parents. They do more than simply share a vision and provide guidance. First and foremost, they convey to their followers that they care. As Theodore Roosevelt wisely said, "People don't care how much you know until they know how much you care."

The best leaders are demonstratively passionate about the success of all employees, even those for whom they feel no personal affinity. Your team must sense that you are there to help them grow and achieve success.

Effective leaders, of course, are also passionate about their business—its core purpose, customers, and key initiatives. They don't necessarily have to be emotional by nature, but they do have to show energy and emotion to those they lead. Employees will feel this emotional vibrancy and thrive off of it. Even "tough love" leaders can and should display positive intent and caring in their mentoring. If the relationship between the leader and the team members is primarily functional, the culture by default will be task-oriented.

We learned in Chapter 2 that a brand is more successful and profitable when it creates an "emotional connection" with its customers. The same is true with leadership. When the leader connects with team members on a deeper level, people will sense this dedication and view their role as important to the overall success of the business.

Leadership DNA

Are exceptional leaders born or made? Do they inherit their leadership skills, or do they acquire them?

People have asked me this question numerous times over the years, and my answer is at odds with popular opinion. I believe that while some leadership attributes can be mentored and learned, the vast majority—especially the foundational ones—are an inherent gift. Some people have them, and other people simply don't. That's why it's so important to do a good job of interviewing and thoroughly vetting candidates when you are filling key positions on your team.

Whenever I'm coaching young children, teaching college students, mentoring and managing employees, interviewing candidates, or otherwise interacting with people, I'm constantly on the lookout for people who have the following five "demonstrable leadership attributes":

- Inspiration: engage with others and inspire them to greatness
- Initiative: be self-starting and accountable for success
- Innovation: dream of possibilities beyond today's realities
- Intelligence: connect dots, spot trends, and define success
- Integrity: do what's right even when no one is looking

As part of my commitment to mentorship (and as an excuse to get back to the college campus), I am a guest lecturer each quarter at the University of Notre Dame's Mendoza College of Business. I'm very impressed with the young men and women coming out of college these days. Most have received and will continue to receive the learning, training, and practical experiences they need to be successful throughout their careers. Even with all of these advantages, however, only a select few will truly excel in their careers and develop into extraordinary leaders who achieve unmatched success.

In my view, success doesn't necessarily entail making lots of money or rising to the top of an organization. I define success as having a game-changing impact on a business, a team, a cause, or some other worthwhile institution or endeavor. Skills, training, experiences, opportunities, the support of team members, and many other factors contribute to such success, but I believe the most important factor is what I call "leadership DNA."

Leadership DNA is the innate skill to visualize the best path forward, see opportunities that others overlook, connect the dots in ways that others cannot, and lead from a place of confidence. These kinds of leaders don't need to ask people to follow them; it just naturally happens.

The evidence of leadership DNA begins to appear as early as grade school. You can spot these blossoming leaders on the playground, in the classrooms, on the athletic fields, in neighborhoods, and in school clubs. They continue to mature as leaders through their high school and college years, as they prepare to enter the adult worlds of art, business, government, medicine, education, and science. I am sure you can name a handful of people you know who have that certain something that engenders the admiration, respect, and loyalty of others. You just want to be around them because you learn from every interaction.

However, no leader, regardless of the depth of their leadership DNA, can achieve and sustain exceptional success alone. Skilled and engaged teams are needed to execute the vision, and good leaders surround themselves with these kinds of people. A mentor once told me, "Your role as a leader is to create the vision, hire people smarter than you are, and then let them spread their wings and be amazing." Outstanding leaders don't have to be—or even want to be—the smartest person in the room. Their primary desire is to help maximize the potential of each team member and the team as a whole. Their job is to notice that their team is losing focus, and then guide them back onto course.

> "Your role as a leader is to create the vision, hire people smarter than you are, and then let them spread their wings and be amazing."

Stages of Leadership

As I have said, I believe great leaders have certain inherent skills. However, leadership is also a process of growth. You can acquire many leadership skills, but if you have not pushed yourself to continually grow as a leader, how can you challenge, mentor and groom future leaders?

Understanding how you lead today and visualizing how you would like to lead tomorrow can facilitate your leadership growth. Use the following four classifications of leadership styles to guide your assessment:

- **Authoritarian Leadership** derives its power from *authority* or *position*. Employees are motivated more by your title than by their desire to achieve. They feel they "have to" follow you, because, after all, you're "the boss."

- **Associative Leadership** derives its power from *relationships*. Employees follow you because they sense you care about and respect them as individuals, not just as employees. Because of this personal connection, they trust you to lead them in the right direction. Some may even have blind faith in you because you make them feel cared for and comfortable.

- **Achievement Leadership** derives its power from *performance*. Employees have confidence in you because in the past you have blazed trails and delivered results. They gladly follow your lead because they want to be part of a winning team.

- **Advancement Leadership** derives its power from *vision*. Employees follow you because you offer them the vision and opportunity to attain higher levels of personal and professional accomplishment than they previously thought possible. They are willing to make sacrifices to achieve this higher level of performance because you inspire them to advance beyond merely "wanting to win" to "wanting to be amazing."

Most inexperienced leaders fit within the authoritarian classification, and perhaps this best describes your style. However, it is up to you to seek opportunities to learn and grow as a leader. Having mentors throughout your career, no matter your position (even CEOs have mentors), helps bring guidance and perspective. I was blessed with great mentors throughout my business career. I took away something from each leader. Mostly things I would like to emulate. But just as importantly, I took away some things I would never want to emulate. Over time you will gain experience, perspective, and skills to grow within the four categories of leadership, even if you don't have a deep level of leadership DNA. Push yourself to grow and develop. You will find that as you evolve, so will your team and business results.

The Power of Engagement

Deep engagement fosters strong commitment. Help team members understand the organization's vision and their individual roles in achieving it. Encourage them to own the vision and "see themselves" as integral to its success. The best way to get employees to own the vision is to directly or indirectly involve them in the development of your strategic plan. Reinforce ownership by holding them accountable for specific results under their control. Chapter 4 talked about the ineffective "top-down, limited-access" process many companies use to develop their strategic plan. No wonder these companies suffer from a lack of employee engagement!

The great majority of companies fail to engage their employees at even an elementary level. In a study commissioned by FranklinCovey and conducted by Harris Interactive, only 44% of the 11,045 adult U.S. workers surveyed said they clearly understood their organization's most important goals. Furthermore, only 19% had clearly defined work goals, and only 9% believed that their work had a strong link to their organization's top priorities.[7] It is virtually impossible for employees to be engaged if they do not see how their work contributes to the overall success of the organization. If they have no emotional connection to their job—if they can see no relevance in their work—they will simply perform a series of tasks while waiting for five o'clock. It's the leader's job to help them make this connection. Failure to do so is a failure of leadership.

It's been my experience that the vast majority of leaders fail to communicate with their employees on a regular basis about

---

7   This study is reported in Christiansen et al., March 2011, Harvard Business Review. https://hbr.org/2011/03/the-big-idea-the-new-ma-playbook

the purpose and strategic direction of their organization. Sadly, many leaders consider the process of building engagement only marginally effective or even a waste of time. But striving for extraordinary engagement is absolutely one of the primary responsibilities of a leader. In fact, I believe it is a leader's single *most* important responsibility and I can cite evidence to support my view. The FranklinCovey study found that companies with a high level of employee engagement achieve up to 57% greater profitability than companies with low engagement. As a business leader, if that data point doesn't hit your radar of "critical to success," I don't know what will!

I've talked with the leaders of hundreds of companies about this engagement issue, and most tell me that they spend lots of time communicating with their employees about goals. But when I dig deeper, I find out that they're talking primarily about the *urgent* tasks on the boss's hot-button list that day, and they're paying little or no attention to the limited number of *critical* issues that will significantly influence the overall success of the business.

> ...companies with a high level of employee engagement achieve up to 57% greater profitability than companies with low engagement.

Take town hall meetings, for example. As the name implies, a town hall meeting is an opportunity for an entire company to come together periodically to share as a "community" about the company's mission, priorities, and performance. When I asked the CEO of one Fortune 1000 company if he had town hall meetings, he confidently replied, "Yes, every quarter our 12 senior leaders meet and talk about the business. Then I ask my leaders to go back to their teams and share the highlights of what we've discussed."

When I surveyed various members of this company's leadership team, I learned that fewer than half of the senior leaders actually passed the information from leadership meetings back to their teams. Several said they used to relay the information, but they stopped because their teams didn't seem interested. In fact, discussions with hundreds of companies lead me to believe that only about half of all companies actually conduct meetings anything close to an effective town hall meeting.

This leader was conducting leadership meetings, not town hall meetings. Now, don't get me wrong, leadership meetings are an important vehicle for informing team members about potential problems and initiating timely interventions. As a matter of fact, I think this leader should have been having them at least monthly. But leadership meetings are not a substitute for town hall meetings, which should occur at least quarterly, ideally monthly.

The above case is not unusual. A "Watson Wyatt Effective Communication 2009/2010 ROI Study Report"[8] found that 50% of employees consider town hall meetings a waste of time. But don't rationalize the lukewarm response to these meetings as justification for you not conducting them. When employees consider town hall meetings boring or irrelevant, the problem is not poor employees; the problem is poor leadership. Strong leaders know how to communicate with their team in a relevant manner that increases engagement, understanding, excitement, and accountability. It's

---

8   Report summary is on Towers Watson Website at https://www.towerswatson.com/en-US/Insights/IC-Types/Survey-Research-Results/2009/12/20092010-Communication-ROI-Study-Report-Capitalizing-on-Effective-Communication

your job as a leader to find the best way to communicate with and engage your team. Never rationalize away the importance and impact of communicating with your team frequently.

What is the best way to communicate with your team? Usually two-way communication is the most effective, according to the Watson Wyatt study. Below are the study's effectiveness rankings for four forms of business communication as a percentage of "achieving full attention" communication:

- Written communication – 15%
- Audio communication in meetings – 23%
- Face-to-face one-way communication – 55%
- Face-to-face two-way communication – 70%

These results clearly indicate that to truly engage employees, you must allow them to have a voice. People like to be talked *with*, not simply talked *to*. The study also found that 90% of the time, in-person meetings build higher levels of trust and engagement than written or audio communication, and that 81% of the time, face-to-face meetings help to reduce confusion and misunderstanding about the path of the company.

In today's business world, where so much management is done from behind a computer, companies are placing less emphasis on communications and engagement. How are you spending your time communicating? How would your team score you on the frequency and value of information you provide?

> ## Homework Assignment
> During one of your usual work weeks, track the hours you spend communicating in each of the communication modes. Assess how effectively you are getting your message across and achieving the full attention and engagement of your team.

In business, as in sports, alignment is key. Returning to the football analogy, when all players collectively and individually are clear about what they are supposed to do on every play, the team will perform dramatically better. If the coach or quarterback doesn't announce the play to all the players before it's run, how do you think the play will turn out? Communication must be frequent, understandable, and relevant. Otherwise, confusion and complacency will set in. As the leader of your organization, you are ultimately responsible for promoting clear and engaging communication.

The Benefits of Accountability

I believe most employees welcome accountability, however, when I say that, the majority of business leaders passionately disagree with me. "My employees don't want to be held accountable," they insist. "They just want to do their job and go home."

But is this really true? I agree that employees don't want to be put under a microscope and micromanaged. (Ironically, leaders who are poor communicators might think micromanagement is necessary, because their followers "just don't understand.") However, employees absolutely do want to feel that their contributions will make a difference in achieving a common vision they consider worthwhile.

With both white-collar and blue-collar jobs, people want to understand how the tasks they perform impact the overall success of the business. Once they understand and buy into the plan, the vast majority

[you can't legitimately hold employees accountable unless you first help them understand the vision and goals of the organization]

want to be held accountable. However, you can't legitimately hold employees accountable unless you first help them understand the vision and goals of the organization and their individual role in achieving them.

In college football, the recruitment of high school athletes is a very competitive process. Year after year, some teams do a really good job of signing up the 4-star and 5-star players. But quite often a team with a host of highly rated athletes will lose to a team whose players had less illustrious high school careers. What allows the team with lesser-rated players to beat a team of all-stars? When you dig deeper, you'll often find that the winning team has a coach with great leadership skills who can create extreme focus and engagement. Because he gets everyone on the team to own the plan, understand his role, and execute his role to the best of his ability (both on and off the field), the team collectively far exceeds expectations.

A similar situation exists in the business world. It's amazing what individual employees can accomplish when they own the vision and work together as a team on initiatives they consider critical to the company's success.

Great leaders excel at putting forth a vision, charting the best path to it, assembling the right team to work for it, and engaging team members at a deep level of ownership and accountability to accomplish it. People readily follow these types of leaders, and the organizations they lead reap amazing benefits from their abilities. When you have a strong and empowered team, you as the leader can then spend more time working "on" the business (focusing on the critical items that move the organization forward) and less time working "in" the business (handling day-to-day routine and urgent tasks).

7

FOCUSING ON THE CRITICAL

Your greatest danger is letting the urgent things crowd out the important.
–Charles E. Hummel

Some people seem to take pride in their *busyness*. "Man, this is going to be another hectic day!" this type of person might announce upon arrival at the office. "Seven meetings, four conference calls, two dozen voicemails to answer, and more than 200 emails to plow through. I don't know how I'll get everything done."

Perhaps you can identify with this individual's predicament. As a business person, you almost certainly have a lengthy to-do list. But have you ever stopped to consider how many of your daily activities truly align with your company's vision and long-term strategy? Do you know what percentage of them will effectively drive you toward the goals you and your organization are committed to achieve?

Busyness: the Enemy of Business

Legendary football coach Lou Holtz once said, "Some people do so little but achieve so much, while others do so much but achieve so little." Which of these two types of people are you? The same thing can be said about companies. Which of these two types of cultures best describes your business?

I strongly believe that most businesses are more complex than they need to be. Even though I've never been to your company, my experiences with hundreds of other organizations prompts me to say with a rather high degree of certainty that this is true of your business, too.

Perhaps the top leadership of your company created this unnecessary complexity, or simply allowed it to creep in. Maybe you're even part of the problem. Regardless of its source, this unnecessary complexity is preventing you and your team from focusing on the truly crucial priorities that will drive the business results you have committed to deliver.

In my 30-plus years of experience in business, I've found it helpful to define and prioritize activities according to the following three categories:

- **Urgent activities** are those that demand your immediate attention. They often greet you when you arrive at work, and several may be on your plate at any one time. You can't magically make them disappear, but you can prioritize them.

They are usually associated with *other people's goals.* Even when their consequences to your business are minimal, you need to promptly handle, delete, or delegate them.

- **Important activities** are those you personally must deal with, given your position and accountabilities. They're usually associated with *your own short- to medium-term goals,* as opposed to other people's goals. Typically you may have two to four of these activities on your plate at one time. Because they can have a substantial and often immediate impact on your organization, you must handle them directly and reasonably quickly.

- **Critical activities** have the potential to completely transform your business or some major aspect of it in an evolutionary, or even a revolutionary, manner. As a leader, critical activities must be at the forefront of your thoughts and actions. They should shape and filter the overarching priorities that guide you and your team. You may have one to two critical activities on your plate at any one time, and they typically have a longer lead time than important activities. The ultimate consequences can be huge if you do not give them adequate attention.

Unless you're unusually diligent about time management, I can say with a high degree of confidence that urgent busywork activities are consuming too much of your available time. Busywork hampers your ability to see and reach for new possibilities, and it keeps your team from focusing on the priorities most important to the success of your business. Clearing away unnecessary complexity and focusing on your role's important items, while leaving time for thinking about critical activities, allows you to accomplish your short- and long-term goals more efficiently and effectively.

> ### Homework Assignment
> Sometime over the next 30 days, track how you spend your time during one "typical" week. The goal is to honestly identify the amount of time you spend doing urgent or routine stuff (working "in" the business) compared to the time you spend thinking about, discussing, or acting on the truly critical items that will measurably impact your business's success (working "on" the business). At the end of the week, look back over your chart to assess your time and be honest with yourself.

Many dieting programs use the above technique, and participants are generally amazed to see how many worthless calories they unwittingly consume. Using an analogous approach, I have charted my hours during a usual workweek several times in my career. I've always found the results enlightening. When you complete this homework assignment, I venture to say that you'll be similarly surprised to see how utterly ineffectively you use your time as a leader.

In dieting, worthless calories are the culprit. In business, busywork is the culprit. Busywork activities always seem important at the time, but actually they're not on the critical path to your company's goals. They're like those worthless calories, except that instead of consuming them, they consume you.

As a leader, you are a *guardian of focus*. It's your responsibility to ensure that everyone understands and is committed to the organization's reason for existence. You must keep people focused on the organization's key business goals and the select few critical initiatives for attaining them. It's your responsibility to refocus your team if it begins to concentrate too much on urgent and important activities at the expense of critical activities.

In the absence of clear goals, employees will guess about what they should and should not do, and fill their days with busywork. They will make assumptions about priorities by creating their own filter, or they will frequently need to interrupt their work to ask their superiors for directions. An

> As a leader, you are a *guardian of focus.*

organization that tries to operate without a plan that specifies goals is like a football team that tries to play a game without a book of specified plays. The result in both situations will be widespread confusion, inaccurate communication, costly delays, and missed opportunities.

An Exercise in Time Management

As was discussed in Chapter 6, the role of an organizational leader is to stretch team members to achieve a vision beyond anything they previously thought possible. And Chapter 3 shared that the role of a market leader is to advance a product category, a market, and ideally an entire industry. These roles can ultimately be fulfilled only by executing critical activities. By definition, critical activities are those select few activities with the potential to dramatically move your business forward.

Planning for critical activities requires dedicated thinking over a period of time. Executing critical activities requires considerable discipline and perseverance. That's why the strategic planning process is so important. It defines the critical activities you will need to undertake to achieve your vision, and it specifies the resources you will need to support these activities.

We all know from experience how difficult it is to carve out time for critical activities. For example, taking care of my body (my personal DNA) is one of my highest priorities, so I make a habit of exercising at least three days a week. I actually put this on my calendar as a commitment, just as I would for any other important meeting. If I don't schedule this as an appointment with myself, other "urgent" activities will begin to crowd out this "critical" activity. I post this appointment publically on my calendar, so others will notice my appointment and know that I am not available during this time. By making my commitment visible, I also hope to inspire others to give high priority to living a healthy lifestyle.

In the same way, we must care for and be publicly dedicated to our business DNA. Just as we need to dedicate time to exercising our bodies, we need to dedicate time to working "on" our business by thinking strategically. Throughout most of my career, I have made critical thinking a personal and team priority, and I have strongly encouraged other leaders and my clients to do the same. When you don't make time to think strategically, the only thing you and your team will make are excuses.

Actually, I must admit that earlier in my career I didn't set aside time for strategic thinking. I devoted the majority of my attention to merely executing tasks. When I executed more tasks than the average person in my role, I felt very successful. That changed when a C-suite mentor reminded me of the importance of quality over quantity.

In response to his challenge, I charted how I spent my days. It turned out I was spending a very small percentage of my week thinking differently about our product category, our target audiences, and our industry. I was disturbed to see how my days (and nights) were devoted to thinking about and handling non-critical activities and tactics. The company was paying me a lot of money for merely ensuring that none of the spinning plates of urgent activities fell to the ground.

I decided to address this deficiency by using the same dedicated time approach I was using with my exercise regimen. I began reserving four to five hours per week for thinking about critical issues. To help enforce my commitment, I reserved a quiet room for my thinking, and I actually put a meeting on my calendar called "Strategic Workout." When people would see that appointment and ask about it, I would tell them it was a *commitment to exercise my brain*, which I considered just as important as my commitment to exercise my body. I knew that if I didn't schedule this time and make it a priority, my strategic thinking sessions would never happen.

As I committed to these thinking sessions and focused our organization's attention on a few critical items, my team could sense the difference in our meetings and in my communications, directives, and actions. They were able to better understand my vision, listen, and engage more receptively to new ideas, and respond more positively and knowledgeably when held accountable.

Soon they began emulating me (as I had emulated my mentor), and on their own initiative they set aside time to focus on the critical items, both individually and collectively. I watched with great satisfaction as team members began delegating or deleting urgent activities so they could focus on important and critical ones.

When I saw my team members curtailing activities that did not align with the overall goals and vision of our business nor merit the commitment of resources, I knew they had grasped the concept. This transformation in setting priorities led to more innovation and positive change across the organization. My team became more confident, focused, engaged, and happy. This new focus also resulted in much stronger business results.

Even though I highly value and continue to execute the discipline described above, sometimes a truly urgent need will arise that causes me to miss one of my strategic workout appointments. However, I will only allow this to happen when the need threatens to impact the whole organization. If I fail to keep an appointment with myself, I will make up the missed hours at some other time in that week.

It's been my observation that the vast majority of people in every organization concentrate on urgent activities. They find it easier and more comfortable to merely stay busy. A definite minority have the courage to think differently and the willingness to set aside time to focus on critical issues. That's why it's so important for you, as the leader, to set the example as a catalyst for change. Once you have set the standard, give your employees the freedom and encouragement to be catalysts for change in their spheres of influence.

If you fail to set your priorities thoughtfully and vigorously, other people's needs will drive your agenda. Distractions will eat up your time and eventually your success. You must learn to stand firm, even if others get upset when *their* "urgent matters" are not getting the immediate attention *they* think they deserve. You can

> If you fail to set your priorities thoughtfully and vigorously, other people's needs will drive your agenda.

help team members understand and accept decisions about priorities by ensuring that everyone is using the same filter. Your unique .1%, vision, and goals that you set in the strategic planning process are your filter. Post them in all offices and conference rooms. When a question arises about how much attention to give to a certain task, this filter will help you improve your decision-making process and your ability to explain your decisions to others.

Filter to Success

Shortly after I assumed the role of Director of Marketing, my team came to me with the proposed marketing plan for the coming year. It listed about two dozen activities, most of which seemed to have very little connection to the company's annual goals. When I asked my team members what filter they had used to prioritize the plan's goals, they told me they had developed the plan in the usual manner of carrying over most of the initiatives from the previous year and adding a couple of new ones.

This approach was clearly inadequate. I put this list of initiatives in a folder and set it aside. I then said to our team, "We're going to postpone our planning meeting until tomorrow. In our next meeting, we're going to use a new process called zero-based planning. No longer will we include activities simply because we've been doing them for years. We're going to wipe the slate clean of all previous initiatives, clear our minds of all preconceived notions, and craft our plan through the filter of the company's overall vision, goals, and strategies."

The following day, I brought a disruptive thinker to the meeting as a planning resource. I knew from experience that this person would stretch us in new directions with challenging questions. I started the meeting by writing on the board the three major goals the company wanted to accomplish during the upcoming year. "These are the three things our senior leadership, the board of directors, our shareholders, and I want to see accomplished," I told our team. "This is our common focus and filter. If we do our part to help achieve these three business goals, the company will be successful, and therefore we will be successful. So our job is simple. We will develop a plan that is aligned with these goals, so we will have the ironclad approach to deliver them."

This fresh, purpose-driven approach focused and motivated the team. It transformed planning from a *painful checklist drudgery* to an *exciting thinking opportunity*. Team members began brainstorming about what types of core marketing initiatives would give us the best opportunity to hit our three business goals. At the end of a great two-day session, we had a fresh perspective on the market and several new ideas for achieving the organization's goals.

I then picked up the folder with the original list of two dozen initiatives, and we asked ourselves, "Which of the projects on this original to-do list are aligned with our three critical business goals? Which ones truly leverage our company's unique .1%? Conversely, which ones are on this list merely because a couple of sales reps are asking for them or because we've been doing them for the past five to ten years?"

As we examined each of the two dozen activities, we found that only six made it to our new list. The rest were out of alignment with our company's three key goals. If we had adopted the original plan, we would have wasted approximately 75% of our resources on items that did little or nothing to move our business toward our vision. We knew that people would be asking for the things we weren't planning to do, but we all agreed that our accountability was achieving the company's goals, not making other employees happy. Senior leadership had empowered me to sidetrack any projects that did not directly support the company's overall goals, and I empowered those under my leadership to do the same.

Saying "No" Is Hard to Do

One of the most difficult challenges for most teams (especially marketing teams) is deciding what *not* to do. I believe that you make more money by saying *no* to things than you do by saying *yes*. The majority of businesses do the same things year after year, simply because they *think* those things are important. Since they don't use zero-based planning, they are in the dark about which initiatives are aligned with their reason for being and their overall goals. Because they don't have the data to show which initiatives really move the needle, they attempt to play it safe by covering all the bases with the same old programs. There's nothing safe about it. This is not strategic planning; it's assembling a checklist of items. It's a waste of time and resources!

When we executed zero-based strategic planning, motivation and job satisfaction dramatically increased. No longer did the members of our team merely come in, chip away at the items on their to-do lists, and leave at five o'clock, unaware of how much their efforts had impacted the business. Instead, they worked with passion, dedication, and creativity on achieving the company's strategic plan, knowing that everything they did was helping to accomplish its goals and actualize its vision. Because they were *owners* of two dozen critical projects instead of *managers* of a long list of urgent and routine projects, they produced superior results. Also, importantly, these incentives were aligned to these business goals.

If we received a request to do a particular marketing program, such as to produce a certain piece of sales literature, our team determined how effectively this project advanced the company's major goals for the year. If it aligned with at least two of the three goals, we usually decided to do it. If it aligned with only one—or none—of the three goals, we definitely wouldn't do it.

> ...you make more money by saying *no* to things than you do by saying *yes*.

We stood firm on these decisions, even when it meant telling the sales department they couldn't have something they had been using for the past ten years.

As we expected, some people didn't like our new approach. For example, as I sat in one particular planning meeting with the sales team, a rep expressed outrage that a piece of literature we had produced for him for several years was not in the budget. This piece cost us $30,000 to produce, so I asked him which of the three goals on the board it supported. After hemming and hawing a bit, he said, "I just need it." When I asked which of his customers used this sales piece, he gave me two names. I reviewed sales data for these two customers and saw that together they contributed less than $10,000 to our company's annual profits. So I asked this sales rep, "If this was your business, would you spend $30,000 to promote a product and market that are not aligned with our three business goals for a profit contribution of less than $10,000?" After ranting for a while, he begrudgingly admitted, "Probably not."

In order to be most effective, the philosophy of focusing on the critical must permeate every level the organization. Just as deficient DNA in the human body can cause health problems, one nonbeliever in an organization—one person who spends his time focused on the urgent instead of on the critical—can derail an initiative and drain energy and focus from the whole enterprise. However, when this philosophy runs deep within the organization, so that the focus is on the organization's unique .1% and the vision and strategy that emanate from it, employees will exercise more initiative and make more insightful and aligned decisions about matters critical to the business's success. The results of this positively transformed culture will be an amazing increase in momentum in business results.

Focusing on the critical will increase the engagement and ownership of your team, which in turn will enhance the productivity and profitability of your business. As we discussed in Chapter 6, companies with a high level of employee engagement achieve up to 57% greater profitability than companies with low engagement. The value of engagement extends out from the company to the market. When you contribute more value to your customers, they can then contribute more value to their customers, creating strong loyalty for your brand.

8

CULTIVATING CUSTOMER EXPERIENCES

The customer experience is the next competitive battleground.

–Jerry Gregoire

In today's world, creating an extraordinary customer experience can be your business' secret weapon. Whether in a B2B relationship or one directly with the end consumer, the customer experience you create will help determine your success. It's so important that according to a Harris Interactive and RightNow survey, at least 55% of adults place more value on the experience a brand offers than on the product itself. Let that sink in and remember how much you invest in R&D for your products. Consider investing some of those dollars, instead, on understanding and creating an extraordinary customer experience. Customers, consumers, channel partners and influencers—whatever way you choose to define your target audience—have a new gauge that determines their intent to buy: customer experience (CX).

As customers become more empowered, it's important that companies understand how the customer experience impacts their business's success. Each year, companies allocate millions of dollars from their SG&A budgets on sales and marketing resources for the purpose of engaging customers and driving them to purchase their products. Unfortunately, many of these companies have very limited knowledge about their customers, including critical insights as to why they actually do (or don't) select their product. As a result, these companies don't fully understand how that massive SG&A spend directly impacts their overall business. To make matters worse, they don't know which triggers to pull to influence future demand.

The expectations surrounding customer experience have dramatically increased. Essentially, customers want—and expect—a deeper and better experience before they commit to products. In addition, 89% of customers stop doing business with a brand after one bad experience. The takeaway—an exceptional customer experience is critical.

> 89% of customers stop doing business with a brand after one bad experience.

However, most companies currently have a false sense of security. According to Bain Consulting, there's a major disconnect between perception and reality. The proof—more than 80% of companies believe they offer a superior customer experience, but only 8% of their customers agree. The opportunity for your company is to understand where the disconnect originates and then set a plan in place to begin filling the gap. Given higher demands and their impact on business results, companies need to start paying attention to the customer experience they create and the impact it can make to the bottom line.

Customer Experiences With B2B Partners

While understanding the consumer is more critical than ever, most products go through the channel, meaning we have very important B2B relationships that we must nurture to make sure our products have placement and that consumers find them. The following story was my initial foray into business relationships and helped define my approach to partnering.

A few weeks into my first sales assignment, after all my training was complete, I was ready to get to selling and demonstrating that I was one of the best sales reps hired to my company. Full of excitement, I was confident I would get a big sale right out of the gate.

Well, I did! I partnered with one of my lumberyard customers to quote on a job to supply the shingles for a large apartment complex. We won this huge order, and everyone in my company was excited for me. But as I was processing the paperwork the night before I was to finalize the sale with my customer, I realized something terrible. I had quoted the order at my cost! I was beside myself. How could I have made such a horrific mistake?

The next morning, I went with much embarrassment to see my customer, Ken Witten, purchasing manager of McClure Lumber in Charlotte, NC. I told him about my mistake and promised to honor the quoted price on the project. Ken sat there without saying a word for several seconds (which seemed like an hour). Then he asked me, "How much margin would you typically make on a job this size?"

"20%," I told him.

"Here's what we're going to do," he continued. "I will give up half of my margin on this order and give it to you. I'll make 10%, and you'll make 10%. We'll learn from this and go forward."

That was when I realized that business isn't about getting whatever you can out of the other guy. It's about creating a long-term partnership. There will always be speed bumps in any relationship, and the value of the relationship is defined by how you manage them. Ken and McClure Lumber became my largest and most loyal customer, and I became McClure's largest partner, all because of the strength of the mutually beneficial partnership we built together.

A Winning Strategy
Most everyone, especially sales reps, will say that price is the biggest barrier in the selling process. But volumes of research say this is far from true. I believe it's very simple. If you focus on price, that's what your customers will focus on. Cutting your prices may win you some short-term business, but sooner or later your competitors will match your cuts. Over the longer term, no one benefits except the customers who receive your discounts. And if your customers resell the products they buy from you, they will also eventually lose, because back-and-forth price cuts and reduced selling prices can turn a previously healthy and profitable product category into a low-margin commodity.

To outperform your competitors and the overall market, approach the market differently. Find your unique .1%, leverage it, and help your customers do the same. Differentiate yourself from your competitors in meaningful ways, and find customers and channels

CULTIVATING CUSTOMER EXPERIENCES

that value your unique differentiation. When you deliver value to your customers, that increases their profits and you won't need to talk about price. Their loyalty to you will increase, ultimately making your business more profitable.

Typically, suppliers provide four things to their customers: price, product, service, and relationship. Most suppliers focus primarily on one or two of these; often they're the wrong ones for greatest profitability.

Price
Price-cutting is a bad sales and marketing strategy because it's the easiest thing for your competitors to match. Besides, once you start talking about price, it's difficult to transition to the other side of the profitability equation: value.

Although Walmart has successfully employed a strategy of consistently low prices for years, few other companies have been able to pull it off. Recently, intense pressure from online retailers like Amazon.com seem to be forcing even Walmart to evolve its strategic retailing approach.

Product
And, product superiority isn't always a guaranteed formula for long-term success. In this age of hyper-speed product development, competitors can catch up quickly. Patents are great, but many are so focused that smart competitors can find ways around them. Therefore, it's best to keep innovating with respect to your product and service platforms, but always attach them to a relevant differentiator that your competitors will have difficulty matching. Find your uniqueness and embed it into the partnerships you build with your customers. Live it every day, so your customers become confident in your brand promise.

Service

Service is another important component of your partnership with your customers, especially in a B2B situation. If you don't fill orders on time and in full, your customers won't have your products to sell to their customers. A satisfactory level of service is usually just the ante to get into the relationship, and once you have developed the relationship, it's merely an expected component of maintaining it. Exercise vision. Rethink your category to find a unique service platform that can set you apart from the competition. Uber and Zappos are two companies that have successfully built their marketing strategy around raising new, and previously unthinkable, expectations of service.

Relationships

Relationships are the fourth important thing you can offer to your customers. When I talk about building relationships, I'm not referring to the social relationships that depend on golfing and fishing junkets, tickets to sporting events, lunches, dinners, and other perks. These may get you a last look, and they may keep your customers loyal for a year (or for as long as it takes them to earn their program incentives for that year). But they won't build loyalty that endures through the ebbs and flows of the market and economy.

> When it comes to influencing buying decisions in today's highly competitive economic environment, helping customers achieve better financial performance will always trump cultivating personal sales relationships.

Even deep friendships with your customers and their families won't engender sustainable loyalty to your business. These personal relationships are important, and good companies and successful salespeople will naturally cultivate them. But in this age of intense competition and economic uncertainty, your customers are increasingly focused on and accountable for stronger business results. When it comes to influencing buying decisions in today's highly competitive economic environment, helping customers achieve better financial performance will always trump cultivating personal sales relationships.

Making Your Customer Successful

My first manager and mentor, Allen Roes, taught me an adage that has benefited me throughout my career. He said simply, "Make your customers more successful, and your own success will naturally follow." He even took that principle one step further by saying, "And the best way to make your customers more successful is by helping them make their customers more successful." In other words, to build lasting, mutually beneficial relationships with your customers, focus on helping your customers' customers.

Helping to make your customers more successful with their customers starts with understanding how your customers' business works. I am continually amazed at how little understanding many companies have about how their target audiences make money and run their business. You must have this fundamental knowledge in order to help them enhance their success.

My company, Interrupt, has been a thought leader in the building products industry for many years, so we are in a great position to deeply understand that industry's comprehensive value chain and where value is extracted at each stage. We realize the importance of having strong distribution channels and a sound sales strategy. We are aware of the value of aligning product needs to the R&D strategy and budget. We know how much a company can favorably impact its bottom line simply by enhancing its capacity utilization by a couple of points, and we understand how a company can dramatically improve its profitability by optimizing its channel and SKU mix.

As we work with our clients and help them develop comprehensive profiles of each of their audiences, we get to know them deeply. We know how to help them create greater profitability for their clients and themselves by maximizing the GMROI (gross margin return on investment) at their big-box customers, for example, and by increasing the close rate for their remodelers. We can teach them how to increase their profits by driving more upgrades at their builders and more leads at their specialty contractors.

We are experts at helping our customers and their customers make more money. This skill makes us highly valuable. Some even consider us indispensable to their success. We aim to provide so much value to our customers that they cannot imagine doing business in the market without us.

The value you deliver to your customers should be relevant to their business needs. Ideally, it should be unique so your competitors can't easily duplicate it. When you understand your customers' businesses as well as they understand them, and you deliver continually evolving products, services, and solutions that help them achieve their goals, you will rarely have to engage in pricing debates or spend time developing price quotes to win their business.

An ancient Chinese proverb says, "When the root is deep, there is no reason to fear the wind." In business we would say, "When your value to your customer runs deep, there is no reason to fear the competition." Deliver more ongoing business value to your customers than they could receive from your competitors, and they will be loyal to you through thick and thin.

A Valued Consultant

The most successful sales organizations are those that challenge their clients to reach stronger business performance. That's what authors Matthew Dixon and Brent Adamson maintain in *The Challenger Sale: Taking Control of the Customer Conversation,* and I for the most part agree. However, I think lead is a better word than challenge, because lead implies a forward action and a cooperative relationship, rather than a potentially adversarial one. So, I would rephrase this philosophy to say, "You will achieve greatest sales success when you lead your customers to stronger business performance by providing them with valuable knowledge and guidance they cannot get from others."

You are being a good advocate on behalf of your customers when you help them evaluate and help advance their traditional ways of doing things. In order to provide this type of leadership, you must know your customers. You must have a deep understanding of their customers, their industries, their markets, how they make money, and how they define success. You need to be aware of national and local market triggers and trends that impact their business, and you should be willing and able to help them exploit market gaps and business opportunities. When you lead your customers in this way—when your salespeople are interacting with their customer contacts more as consultants than as sales reps—you are practicing "consultative selling."

Consultative selling is a popular but often misunderstood and misused term. Many companies think they are doing consultative selling when, in reality, they're simply offering more product training to their customers in an attempt to sell more products. It's good to give your customers in-depth information about the products you want them to buy, but don't call that consultative selling. It's simply self-serving selling. Consultative selling is the process of leading your customer to greater success by sharing your exclusive business knowledge, data, and expertise. I deliberately said business knowledge to make a distinction from product knowledge. All good salespeople share knowledge of their products. I'm talking about sharing knowledge about the market, industry trends, category benchmarks, and other things that can help your customers understand how their business performance stacks up, with the ultimate goal of leading them to outperform their market.

According to the dictionary, a consultant is an "advisor who leads from a place of knowledge on a certain topic to help another party get to a more successful place." Sales reps engage in consultative selling when they help their customers create a sustainable and more profitable business. In the course of your day-to-day consultative interactions, you will collect additional valuable information and data that will continue to build your knowledge portfolio. By freely sharing this information with your customers, you can help navigate their businesses (and ultimately yours) down a more successful path.

When you are knowledgeable about how your customers' businesses work, and you demonstrate that you want to help them make more

CULTIVATING CUSTOMER EXPERIENCES

money, they will begin to see you as a "business partner," instead of as a mere vendor. Any company can be a vendor, but very few have the dedication and knowledge platform to be a true business partner. If you give your customers a discount or take them on a trip as a reward for purchasing a certain volume of products or for earning points in some program, they may be yours for a year or for however long it takes them to earn that incentive.

> Any company can be a vendor, but very few have the dedication and knowledge platform to be a true business partner.

On the other hand, when you help them build their business, you will earn their loyalty for life. As your customers become more profitable, you become more valuable (and profitable). It's a win-win proposition.

Enabling a Consultative Sales Process

How do you transition your organization to consultative selling? I suggest taking the following five steps:

1. Adopt the philosophy that you are successful only when your customers are successful. Ask your customers how they judge their success, so you can measure your progress within their success metrics. This should be prominent on your monthly dashboard.

2. Measure and incentivize the performance of your sales team and your marketing team around the success of your customers. This will transform and align the communication between your sales reps and their customers, and it will promote cooperation between your sales team and your marketing team. Focusing more on the success of your customers will allow you to focus less on your own success, which will take care of itself.

3. Train your sales and marketing teams to ask good questions of their customers. When they understand how their customers' businesses operate, how they make money, how they sell and market, and where they are experiencing problems, they will be better able to serve as consultants to them. Below are some good questions to ask.

- What is your definition of success?

- What are your top three strategic initiatives?

- What are the major pain points in your business (i.e., what keeps you up at night)?

- What are the levers you can pull to most increase profits?

- What are the barriers that keep you from closing more sales or upgrades more quickly?

- What is your definition of the optimal customer or project?

- What keeps you from growing 20, 30, 50%?

4. Arm your sales and marketing teams with knowledge, data, and innovative tools for coaching their customers in a professional and consultative manner that far exceeds anything the competition can offer. When I ran the sales department, my sales reps were equipped to give their customers advice about many aspects of their business.

For example, they might counsel their customers by saying something like, "Approximately 27% of the products sold in your marketplace are premium (best) products, and only 17% of your sales are in that category. Also, your close rate is 25% under the industry average. Let us craft tools and training for your team, so you can capture more of that unrealized profit opportunity."

5. Create a structured process to ensure that all team members—especially those in sales, marketing, and customer service—communicate messages to your customers that are consistent and aligned at every touch point. After nurturing and bringing in business, there is nothing worse than having that customer relationship derailed by a faulty process. Keeping a customer should be the easy part!

Without a structured process, sales reps tend to sell the products most familiar to them in ways most comfortable to them. They'll gravitate to the channels and customers they prefer spending time with, and they'll say what they personally think is important. From a companywide standpoint, excessive freedom results in confused messages, inconsistent brand representation, and subpar sales results.

Enhance your consultative selling skills by exercising good listening skills. As you listen to the answers your customers give to your questions (step 3), you'll gain valuable information about industry trends, effective solutions to problems, and other business matters. You can then draw on this warehouse of knowledge when consulting with other customers, always being careful to protect confidentialities. The more you consult, the more knowledge you gain, and the more effective you become as a consultant. Consultative selling is a powerful, self-reinforcing process!

When your company practices consultative selling, your sales reps essentially become business partners to your customers (or at least that's how your customers should feel). Your reps will focus on helping customers grow their business, rather than on simply selling them products and keeping them happy. Imagine how appreciative your customers will be when your salespeople begin to advise them about such issues as where their sales process is suboptimal, how they can increase the ROI on their marketing spend, where they are leaving money on the table, how they can close sales more quickly, and how they can optimize their more profitable products. Do you think this would create more loyal customers than the golf outings you sponsor each year? Absolutely!

Yes, I know price is important. But it's really about profitability. There are two sides to profitability: the cost side and the value achieved side. If you focus primarily on the cost side, your customers will focus there, too. If you focus on the value achieved side, you will still have a certain percentage of customers who will hassle you over price (studies show it will be approximately 10%), but you can and should shed most of this over time. The good customers—the kind you want to keep—will pay you fair prices for the value you provide, and they will keep coming back.

> There are two sides to profitability: the cost side and the value achieved side. If you focus primarily on the cost side, your customers will focus there, too.

You may still want to take certain customers on golfing outings and fishing trips from time to time, but you won't have to rely on these social excursions as sales tools. Although it's nice to give your customers memorable occasions, your first priority should be to help them build a more sustainable, profitable business.

Many customers start their conversation about price because it's an easy initial point of focus. When that happens, change the conversation by stating "what you are really concerned with is profitability." Seek to understand their business and identify how you can uniquely contribute to its success. Educate them by connecting the dots about how you can provide value that addresses their points of pain and enhances their business results. It's your job to demonstrate reasons why they should partner with you instead of with your competition.

A Selling Approach That's Through the Roof

Here's a story that illustrates the principles outlined above. Early in my career, I sold roofing shingles to independent dealers and lumberyards throughout the Southeast. Most of my dealers had a Lowe's store nearby, and all of these stores sold exactly the same shingles at considerably lower prices than my dealers could charge. In fact, Lowe's prices to its retail customers would sometimes be lower than my prices to my dealers. This became an ongoing emotional issue. Almost every time I walked into one of my dealer's stores, I would be greeted by the employees waving the latest weekly sales flyer from Lowe's.

One of my top lumber dealers was New Hope Lumber in Gastonia, NC. The general manager there was Dan Pope. With a confident and mild disposition, he taught me a lot in my early days as a sales rep. One day I was in Dan's office when he got a phone call from a roofing contractor who had recently placed an order with his company for shingles to be delivered to one of his jobs. The yelling on the other end of the line was so loud that I could hear every word. After listening for a few seconds, Dan winked at me and put the call on speaker. The man on the phone was one of New Hope's largest roofing contractors. He went on for at least ten minutes about how Lowe's price for a square of shingles was $2 (about 10%) lower than New Hope's. "You're fleecing me!" he yelled. "You're going to put me out of business. You need to match Lowe's price, or you'll lose my business forever. So, what are you going to do, Dan?" Dan looked at me again, this time with a grin. Then he said to this contractor, "Tommy, I appreciate the call, and I do very much appreciate your business. Yes, we already know about Lowe's prices. Yes, they are $2 per square lower than ours in today's paper. But no, we will not lower our price. I am happy to cancel the order you have with us if that is your desire, but before I do, let me remind you of what else you will be cancelling that Lowe's does not offer."

Dan paused for a few seconds. Then he continued: "Say 'goodbye' to rooftop delivery. Bid 'farewell' to someone who deeply understands your business and is willing to provide the credit you need to stretch between jobs. Say 'adios' to my throwing two bundles in my truck at lunchtime and driving 10 miles to your jobsite so your crew can keep on working. Say 'sayonara' to the homeowner leads we send your way and the samples and training we provide to your new crew members, not to mention the pizza, donuts, and coffee your crew consumes at our shop each day. So, Tommy, if that is not all worth $40 a roof, I will go ahead and cancel these 20 squares that are scheduled to your jobsite."

After several seconds of silence, Tommy's voice, now monotone and contrite, comes over the phone: "Just make sure they are delivered by 3:00 pm today."

I've been forever grateful for what Dan taught me that day. In just a few minutes, I gained a greater appreciation for the value I bring to my customers. I learned the importance of taking my customers' eyes off of price and focusing them on the relevant benefits of partnering with us. After gaining valuable perspective from that experience, whenever my customers complained about our prices, I explained to them how the value of our services aligned with their needs, and how this value more than justified our prices. Thanks, Dan! Next time the donuts and pizza are on me. Enable your customers by helping them become more successful with their customers. Focus on value, not price. Measure your success by how well you have helped your customers meet their business goals and outperform their market. Build strong relationships with them by being a consultant and a true business partner, versus a mere sales rep or supplier. Everyone sells products. Very few sell value. When you do these things, you will have customers who are loyal for life. Not to mention, a much more profitable business. Loyal customers also make executing your plan much easier because your relationship starts from a place of confidence and trust.

9

EXECUTING FOR SUCCESS

Success doesn't necessarily come from breakthrough innovation but from flawless execution. A great strategy alone won't win a game or a battle; the win comes from basic blocking and tackling.

–Naveen Jain

Your job as a business leader is to deliver results. In the final analysis, your performance will be judged and your compensation will be determined by the business metrics you achieve. So how do you ensure that you and your organization fulfill and even surpass your commitments to your senior leadership and stakeholders?

The previous chapters discussed a number of new and different principles and approaches for achieving greater business success. All are built on the foundation of leveraging your unique .1%. I hope many of these concepts will be useful to you as you cast your vision and develop your strategic plan. But developing your plan is in many ways the easiest part. The next and more challenging step is to *flawlessly execute* your plan.

In their March 2015 *Harvard Business Review* article titled "Why Strategy Execution Unravels—and What to Do About It,"[9] authors Donald Sull, Rebecca Homkes, and Charles Sull state that "a recent survey of more than 400 global CEOs found that executional excellence was the number one challenge facing corporate leaders in Asia, Europe, and the United States. It headed a list of some 80 issues, including innovation, geopolitical instability, and top-line growth." The authors went on to say that "studies have found that two-thirds to three-quarters of large organizations struggle to implement their strategies."

My own experience confirms this. The majority of executives I talk with tell me that failure to execute is their organization's biggest barrier to success. Business leaders will provide many rationalizations for missing their plan, but in the end these reasons all boil down to some form of poor execution.

I believe there are three primary enemies of flawless execution: lack of engagement, insufficient resource allocation, and poor alignment. These villains are always trying to creep in and undermine your business success.

Engagement and Allocation Drive Execution
Successful execution starts with successful engagement, and successful engagement starts with understanding. If team members

9   Retrieved from https://hbr.org/2015/03/why-strategy-execution-unravelsand-what-to-do-about-it

don't understand your plan and their role in it, they cannot be "all in" to make it reality. The odds will be stacked against success even before you start.

Strong engagement creates a sense of ownership. When your team members "own" the plan, they will execute it purposefully as opposed to merely halfheartedly. They will focus more attention on the critical goals that drive progress, and less attention on immediate tasks that soak up time. Previous chapters discussed how to create this sense of ownership, and I'll offer more guidance in this chapter.

Once your team is engaged, allocate resources wisely. Nearly 90% of the leaders surveyed in the Harvard study said that poor allocation of resources is one of the major reasons for initiative failures. That's a shocking statistic! Resource allocation and investment analysis should be an important part of your strategic planning process.

The majority of executives I interact with admit that if they could only fix their execution issues, their profitability would dramatically increase. And yet, after spending several weeks behind closed doors creating a strategic plan, many of these same executives will try to execute it with inadequate resources managed by personnel with the wrong sets of skills.

In today's economy, I understand organizations must continually attempt to optimize operational efficiencies by striving to do more with less. But many are being penny-wise and dollar-foolish by skimping on their investment in new opportunities, innovation, and growth. Countless times I have seen companies inadequately staff an important project by having a handful of people dedicate

10% of their time to it. Such weak commitment will almost certainly ensure subpar performance, and it will definitely rule out incredibly "unthinkable" results over and above your plan.

Many companies place far too much emphasis on limiting headcount costs. They just don't seem to appreciate the value of investing $200,000 of headcount in a $10 million opportunity. If you deem an initiative is critical, then appropriately resource it. If it's not critical, take it off your list. As we discussed in the previous chapter, an important part of leadership is defining the *few critical* things to accomplish. An equally important part is defining what *not* to do. Don't dissipate the energy of your organization by resourcing a project with small pieces of people who have other major priorities.

Eight out of ten managers in the aforementioned Harvard study said their companies were too slow to exit declining businesses and kill unsuccessful initiatives. Often the indecisive leaders of these businesses will continue to fund a project just because it's a senior leader's pet idea, or because it's been on the to-do list forever. Don't fall into this trap! Have the alertness and backbone

> If a project is critical to your success, resource it accordingly. If it is not, either reprioritize it or kill it.

to know when you should redeploy resources from marginally worthwhile initiatives to more profitable and sustainable business opportunities. Then summon the courage to actually do it.

An initiative is either critical or it is not. Use your vision and strategic plan as your filter when making decisions about funding new and existing initiatives. If a project is critical to your success, resource it accordingly. If it is not, either reprioritize it or kill it.

Alignment Is Crucial

In sports, the most successful coaches have an exceptional ability to communicate vision and expectations. They can take players of any skill level and mold them into a cohesive team that works in unity to achieve the desired end goal. In the same way, the most successful business organizations ensure that all team members understand the plan and are 100% aligned with it, so they're always executing with the end goal in mind.

To again cite the Harvard study, when researchers asked corporate managers to identify their single greatest challenge to executing their company's strategy, 40% stated misalignment with the organization's goals, while 30% cited failure to coordinate across units.

In my experience, the two key functional areas that are rarely aligned with each other are sales and marketing. It just so happens that these two areas are the most critical to the successful execution of a company's brand and business plan. Solving the alignment issues between sales and marketing will dramatically increase your probability of success. Toss in the alignment of your operations team, and you will be on a trajectory for outstanding performance.

I've sat in on numerous meetings with the sales and marketing teams, and many times the tension between them was thick enough to cut with a knife. After marketing presented a new campaign, program, or collateral approach, I've heard sales reps saying under their breath, "How the heck did marketing think this up? It will never work with my customers. What a waste of money!" At the same meeting I might hear the marketing people say, "These sales guys won't use these great programs we've developed. They will just create their own out in the field and bastardize our brand while doing it."

Misalignment among marketing, sales, and operations typically surfaces as a blame game. I've been in leadership roles in all three of these functional areas, and today I'm a consultant to the leaders of these areas for my clients, so I'm intimately familiar with how the dialogue goes. Here are a few stereotypical examples:

- **Marketing leaders** may say, "Why can't those *sales* reps execute *their* sales plans properly, and why are those *operations* people always so late and over budget with *their* product introductions?"

- **Sales reps** might complain, "Why don't those *marketing* people make *their* programs and materials more usable in our market, and why does *operations* keep letting our customers down with *their* quality and service issues?"

- **Operations leaders** join in with something like, "Our inventory is stacking up! Why can't those *sales* reps make *their* forecasts, and why can't those *marketing* gurus do a better job developing *their* marketing programs to push more product?"

In these conversations, I will repeatedly hear the word "their." It's amazing ("shocking" might be a better word) how rarely I will hear the word "our." The hypothetical sales, marketing, and operations teams quoted above obviously are not working collaboratively. Perhaps that's because their goals and expectations are misaligned, as is usually the case in reality. To make matters worse, in most companies these three functional areas are separated into three departments with different physical locations, philosophies, cultures, and leadership styles. All of this causes constant friction between employees internally and continual confusion with customers externally, ultimately resulting in poor execution before it gets out the door.

Unaligned performance measurements and incentives will exacerbate the problem. For example, marketing may be incentivized to stay within its budget and deliver certain identified programs. Sales might be incentivized to hit revenue bogies, usually without regard to channel or product mix. And operations might be incentivized to achieve efficient operations, a good safety record, and low inventory costs. These disparate goals do not promote unity of action. In fact, they are more likely to undermine it. To overcome this foundational misalignment, leadership must coordinate metrics and incentives, so they encourage achievement of common goals critical to the company's success.

Proactive Collaboration

I believe that strong collaboration among marketing, sales, and operations is possible in both large and small organizations. But instilling a sense of ownership that supports this kind of collaboration can be a challenge. A sense of ownership typically won't spontaneously develop; you must promote it by aligning these three functional areas around common critical priorities. So all the wheels are turning the same direction at the same speed.

 One effective way to create ownership is to engage the sales team in the marketing planning process. On major initiatives, for example, we typically ask our clients to appoint one to three sales champions from

among their sales reps to ensure that planning remains relevant. These champions will participate in planning conference calls and provide continuous input to the marketing process as liaison to their sales rep peers. We like to have sales champions along with the marketing people present new programs to the sales force at national sales meetings, because it generates a much higher level of collaborative ownership. And as was mentioned earlier, greater ownership translates into better execution.

During a typical year, most marketing teams spend 95% of their time in their headquarters, with some time out at a few trade shows. But such limited time in the field won't give them an accurate sense of the market reality. Marketing leadership should require their teams to spend 15% to 20% of their time traveling with sales reps, attending customer meetings, making store visits, and attending industry forums. The marketing people need this exposure to understand the realities of the industry and trends as they put together marketing plans and tactics.

To promote mutual understanding, we sometimes have marketing "pitch" a product to sales, and then we have sales "pitch" that product back to marketing. This usually results in two very different styles, and management can cherry pick from the best aspects of each.

Starting From Scratch

Many marketing teams make the mistake of doing the same things over and over again without evaluating the ROI. For instance, they produce the same promotional pieces year after year, merely because sales reps insist they need all of these tools to be successful. This is why virtually all marketing teams have way too many pieces of sales and marketing collateral to manage, update, and fund. We have found from conducting numerous marketing audits that most marketing teams have at least 30% more marketing elements than they need to achieve their goals. These elements persist year after year, adding unnecessary complexity to the business and creating a drag on resources and profits, simply because management hasn't created organizational focus and therefore the team doesn't know where to start cutting.

Most companies need to do a much better job of aligning their marketing plans with their next year's business goals. Marketing and sales champions should come together annually to audit their tools and right-size their offering. We also recommend to our clients that they proactively cut 10% to 20% of their existing sales and marketing pieces *each* year to keep their portfolio fresh and focused on current goals and leveraging new ways to engage. As we discussed in Chapter 4, marketing teams should also start at a zero-based budget to ensure that their plans are aligned with their business strategy.

Some companies are driven by sales, and in other companies marketing is in the driver's seat. Imbalance either way creates disharmony and suboptimal performance. You will have the best chance to maximize your business results (and reduce your stress levels) with a collaborative plan that is 100% aligned with the organization's business goals and with the activities and expectations of sales and marketing.

What Gets Paid for Gets Done (Sometimes)

People will execute on what others hold them accountable to accomplish or pay them to do. Therefore, the best way to motivate your sales and marketing teams to achieve your organization's goals is to create rewards and performance review accountabilities around the key strategies and initiatives that come out of the planning process. I am shocked at how many companies have dramatically different goals for each of their functional areas. No wonder they lack strong, collaborative, and focused execution!

Many sales and marketing professionals (those who are executing many of the business strategies) admit to me that incentives have little to do with their ultimate performance. Why? Because their incentive plans are not clear and accessible. Your sales and marketing teams need to understand what they are expected to do and how their work attaches to the overall success of the business. Then they need to receive feedback on how they are performing month to month compared to expectations.

Why Most Incentives Fail

Incentives that are difficult to understand or that rely on complicated measures of success can do more harm than good. The confusion they create can actually work as a *disincentive.* I have heard hundreds of sales and marketing professionals say something like, "I have no idea what my payout will be this year. I just wait until the payouts happen to see what I will get." These kinds of confusing incentives don't drive focused execution externally with customers or internally with employees. They're a waste of both time and money.

> Incentives that are difficult to understand or that rely on complicated measures of success can do more harm than good.

Designing an incentive plan aligned with your organization's goals is only the first step. After introducing the plan, you must reinforce it by communicating a clear and consistent message that focuses on the *critical* outcomes it's designed to promote. If you get distracted and begin to place more emphasis on *urgent* day-to-day matters, your employees will feel pulled in two directions, and your incentive plan will lose its effectiveness.

Even the most powerful incentive plan can't get people to perform beyond their abilities. Before you promote people into new positions or alter their responsibilities, make sure they have the requisite skills to do the job. Sales reps who are highly successful in the field won't necessarily perform well as sales leaders or marketing managers. Regardless of the incentives, they will have a difficult time achieving their goals if they lack the abilities. When promoting people, make sure they are a fit for the position, are well trained, and have clear accountabilities.

The Right Motivation

People have different skill sets, temperaments, and desires. They also have different preferences, in part because of their job positions and life circumstances. Take these differences into account as you determine how to assign people to roles and how to motivate them with rewards and recognition. Your company will have only a few goals (e.g., to achieve a certain profit level), but you will have many options for influencing behaviors to achieve these goals. An important step in creating a successful incentive program is determining what triggers will best promote outstanding performance. Base rewards on more than individual accomplishments. Take into account how individuals positively impact the advancement of other team members and the team as a whole.

Never cap incentives that promote behaviors financially beneficial to the company. With sales commissions and other incentives that promote organizational profitability, unlimited incentives are in the company's best interest, because the better employees perform, the more profit the company will make. It does sometimes get tricky when the company's production capability bumps up against capacity, but that's a problem the company should handle separately from the incentive issue. If you cap people, they will play the game of bringing in business only when it benefits them.

Most sales incentives are aimed at the top 20% of performers. These people, however, are already highly motivated; they're wired that way. That's why the same sales people win the sales contests time after time. The opposite is true for the bottom 20% of performers. They may never achieve at a high level, regardless of the incentives. That's why most pharmaceutical companies cut the bottom 10% of their sales forces each year. Most companies have a hard time firing their underperfomring sales reps. This hurts the company immensely. If you believe these lackluster performers will hurt your business when they leave, you have a bigger problem of value then you know.

You can best move the needle of overall business performance by motivating the middle 60% of the pack. Design your incentive programs to drive results within this group. Pay less attention to the ones who will perform very well or very poorly, regardless of incentives.

Here are some key points to remember when developing a successful incentive program:

- Communicate the strategic plan so all concerned understand it and buy into it. This is the baseline and filter to which all other goals should be aligned.

- Set clear and easy-to-measure goals for the overall business, each division, each team, and each individual.

- Specifically align an individual employee's goals with the strategic plan, and establish clear measurements of progress (milestones) that are readily accessible.

- Provide overall business performance reporting for the collective team in monthly town hall meetings.

- Meet with each individual quarterly to discuss actual performance with respect to his or her personal goals and impact to the company.

- Avoid the "one-size-fits-all" approach. When possible, customize your plan to trigger the key points of leverage for specific functional areas and individuals.

- Make sure employees have the necessary skills and training required for their roles.

- Aim your incentives primarily at enhancing the performance of the middle 60% of your team.

- Maintain constant communication and alignment among all leadership levels, focusing on the organization's critical goals.

Small Things Mean the Most

The strongest incentive is also the easiest and least costly to provide. It's a simple expression of recognition. Small things—a handshake from the CEO, a handwritten letter from the team leader, a simple recognition at the beginning of a meeting—can be amazingly impactful. Take time to recognize the teams and individuals who have had wins along the way.

Get to know your team members so you understand what makes them tick. Then you will be able to customize your recognitions to make them more personal. Thoughtful little gestures like sending a wine basket to the hotel room of an employee who's on a family vacation, enrolling an employee in a weekly art class she has always wanted to take, or fixing the dent in an employee's new car can have a powerful impact, not only on the employee, but on the whole organization. These small gestures will help you to more powerfully engage your team. Stronger engagement will lead to more focused and effective execution, which will ultimately produce the business results you promised to achieve in your plan. With better results come bigger incentive payouts for your team and stronger employee retention. It's a self-reinforcing process.

Simplifying Success

Recently I was sitting in on a client's sales meeting when the new CEO excitedly stood up at the beginning of the meeting and exclaimed to the 30 seasoned sales reps in attendance, "Our strategy is to grow our business by $100 million over the next two years, and you are just the team to do it!" For several seconds, the room was eerily silent. Eventually, one of the VPs started a slow clap, and others reluctantly joined in.

That clearly wasn't the reaction this CEO was looking for. It's not that this sales team lacked the desire or the ability to grow the business. They simply did not connect strongly with the CEO's goal. Business goals that stretch the organization create excitement, but employees must believe they're achievable. They need to relate to their impact on them before they can own them.

After dinner that night, while hanging around the bar (where I usually get the most honest and colorful scoop), I listened to several off-the-cuff comments from the team. Members of the marketing team said something like, "We don't even have enough marketing dollars and time to execute our current strategy, so how the heck are we going to achieve his lofty goal?" A couple of the sales people chimed in, "Where did he pull that $100 million figure from? That's a huge number!" Another added, "Every new leader comes in and announces some sort of new strategy. I guess we will just have to wait and see how this one plays out."

Later I grabbed the CEO and his leadership team and told them about the confusion and complacency I had witnessed. The CEO admitted that he was disappointed, even frustrated, at the unenthusiastic response his new vision received from the sales and marketing teams.

"Let's stand back and make this $100 million goal real to them," I suggested. "They need to see it as relevant to their goals before they will own it, and they're the ones who have to execute it in the market." The CEO and his leadership team nodded in agreement, so I began writing the following on a napkin:

Total market for product category: $10B

This company currently had a 5% share of the market, or sales of about $500M per year. Selling $100M more per year would be a 20% increase over what they were currently doing. That seemed like a lot, but I skipped over that number. Instead, I wrote the following:

$100M = a 1% market share increase

"We only need to capture an additional 1% of the total market of $10 billion to meet the $100M goal," I pointed out. "Our products are not a good fit for the entire market, so let's focus on the best target market fit for our semi-custom products." After discussion, we decided that our products were best aligned with regional home builders construction practices and offerings. From our experience, we knew that these types of companies built an average of 450 homes a year.

I then drilled down to help us understand how many new customers we needed. We knew that on average these builders utilized about 27 units per home, with an average value to our company of $250 each. This meant that each home was worth approximately $6,750 to us (27 x $250). Since on average each builder would use our products in 450 homes per year, each regional builder prospect was worth around $3 million dollars to us. Therefore, we merely needed to convert 33 new builders to reach our incremental goal of $100 million. Since the company had 30 sales reps, we could meet our goal if each rep brought in approximately one new builder.

By this time, my napkin looked something like this:

That night the leadership team put together a simple slide to demonstrate this simplified math, and the next morning we presented it in the meeting. Our goal clicked with the audience of sales, marketing, and operations professionals. The room came alive with excitement and pride, and ideas started flowing. The sales and marketing people became engaged in the strategy and even started taking ownership of it, now that they could see themselves impacting the desired results. At lunch, conversations were very different from the night before. I heard things like, "Well, 1% share seems doable," and, "I can definitely get one builder, maybe even two."

Instead of marketing to all 72,000 builders in the U.S., we needed to target only the 4,500 regional builders that fit the profile attributes we developed. First, they had to align with the regions where the company played, and second, they had to build the style of homes that used the company's products. Using digital technology to focus our efforts, we would deliver highly qualified leads for the sales team for a very reasonable marketing spend. The marketing team liked this more focused approach. I heard comments like, "Now we can do a better job of putting the right amount of marketing dollars focused in the right places."

> Strong alignment can be your most powerful tool for achieving success.

This is one example of the process for simplifying your vision of success and aligning your sales and marketing teams around one common, critical goal. Strong alignment can be your most powerful tool for achieving success. I guarantee that your performance metrics will improve when your sales and marketing (and operations) teams

183

begin to work more collaboratively toward common critical goals. And focusing recognition and rewards around these common goals will dramatically increase your execution success. All of this adds up to making it simple for your team and business to succeed.

10

DOING BUSINESS WITH BACKBONE

The principles I've presented in this book can help you advance your team, your business, and your industry. They are wrapped around the proposition that you will be most successful when you stand out in the sea of sameness and leverage that unique .1% of your business that dramatically differentiates you from the competition.

In these pages, I have challenged you to step back from the current chaos of day-to-day urgencies and focus on the critical issues that have the greatest impact on your success. I've encouraged you to become confident in your business' "reason to exist" by ensuring that it truly offers something of exclusive value to those it serves. And, I've suggested that you define the success of your business through the prism of the experience your brand creates for your customers and to measure your customers' success based upon winning, only when your customers win.

In these pages, I strived to push your thinking beyond the familiar and comfortable. My goals were to help you to see possibility in a new way, to better understand how a true market leader acts, to evolve your personal leadership skills to a new level, and to better appreciate the value of an engaged and focused team. I hope I have succeeded by helping you to become more comfortable with being uncomfortable.

This book is about having the resilience and the vision to lead with force in the midst of discomfort. It's about making amazing things happen, in spite of internal and external pushback. Whenever I hear my kids, friends, employees, and even my fellow business leaders say, "I wish...," I want to cry out in opposition. Wishing for something is a passive action devoid of vision and accountability. It indicates a reluctance to accept responsibility, seize opportunities, meet challenges head on, and achieve goals no matter what. Instead, commit to saying "I will."

Extraordinary success requires the courage to disrupt yourself, to think and lead from a different place. It requires the backbone to diverge from the norm. The quote below by Clementine Paddleford is my favorite for both business and life. It has been displayed on my desk for more than 25 years. As I close this book, I leave these words with you as both an encouragement and a challenge:

**Never grow a wishbone where
your backbone should be.**

GLOSSARY

.1%: The unique element of a business that dramatically differentiates it from its competition, thereby creating differentiated value for its customers.

Business backbone: The courage to think and lead a business on a path that diverges from "business as usual."

Consultative selling: The process of leading customers to greater business success by sharing the selling company's unique and comprehensive business knowledge, data, and expertise.

Culture of possibility: An organizational culture that embraces opportunities as though failure is not an option.

Demand creation: The process of creating incremental demand for an industry, thereby making the overall industry pie bigger.

De-maturing a market: Rethinking and repositioning a mature market at the end of its life cycle to create the beginning of a new life cycle.

Demonstrable leadership attributes: The four key attributes of *inspiration, initiative, innovation*, and *intelligence* that successful leaders deliver to their teams.

Evolutionary leadership levels:
1. **Authoritarian** leadership: derives its power from *authority* or *position*.
2. **Associative** leadership: derives its power from *relationships*.
3. **Achievement** leadership: derives its power from *performance*.
4. **Advancement** leadership: derives its power from *vision*.

Leader's trap: The trap of ultra-conservatism and innovation stagnation that companies with leading market share fall into when they become so afraid of losing their dominant position within an industry that they prioritize market stability over market leadership.

Leadership DNA: The innate skill to visualize the best path forward, see opportunities that others overlook, connect the dots in ways that others cannot, and lead from a place of confidence and care.

Level of activities:
- **Urgent activities** are those that demand the leader's immediate attention. Several may be on the leader's plate at any one time.
- **Important activities** are those the leader must deal with personally due to his or her position and accountabilities. They're usually associated with the leader's short- to medium-term goals, as opposed to other people's goals. Typically two to four of these activities will be begging for the leader's attention at any one time.
- **Critical activities** have the potential to transform the business or some major aspect of it in an evolutionary, or even a revolutionary, manner. Successful leaders usually focus on one to two critical activities at any one time. They typically have longer lead times than important activities.

Market leader: A company that demonstrates market leadership, which is not necessarily the company with the largest volume share.

Market leadership: The process of advancing a category and ultimately the overall industry to a higher level of performance and impact.

Possibility market: The entirety of the market that logically (through data) can utilize the category solution. The holistic market that an industry can ultimately capture, not merely the share of the market that is currently being captured.

Possibility share: The share percentage of the possibility market that a company has currently secured.

Reason to exist: The justification for existence a company earns by offering something unique that customers can't live without and that the market truly needs to be more successful.

Sea of sameness: A competitive environment in which all companies look, sound, and act virtually alike.

Simplifying success: The process of simplifying the business's vision of success and aligning each member of its sales and marketing teams around a common critical organizational goal.

Strategic planning: The crafting of a plan that becomes part of the fabric of the organization and serves as a guide and filter for all conversations, activities, and decisions.

Strategic workout: A specifically scheduled commitment a leader makes to exercise his or her brain to think more strategically about the business.

Zero-based planning: Planning from a beginning budget of zero by ignoring the previous year's initiatives and filtering each new idea through the new strategic plan.

Bill Rossiter CEO & Principal, Interrupt

Bill Rossiter has helped hundreds of companies outperform their industry by teaching them how to escape the sea of sameness and stand out by thinking and acting differently. In *Diverge,* he reveals unique techniques to improve branding, strategic planning, team engagement, and ultimately profits. The innovative insights packed into this easy-to-read book can help dramatically transform your organization's culture and business results, and enhance your own personal success. Use it as a guide to disrupt yourself.